ADVANCED P

MW00532223

The "Yes, And" Business Evolution

Tracy's thoughtful and creative approach to revolutionizing how we work and stay in connected, meaningful relationships with our colleagues is innovative, compelling, and, most of all, fun. She artfully translates the tenets of improv to impart important lessons for leadership and teamwork, where we start from a place of active listening and true understanding without defensiveness to spark lasting, positive change in ourselves and those we work with. The illustrative case studies give you a glimpse of the outcomes you can expect—and are just the beginning of what is achievable for you if you apply these principles. I highly recommend this book to anyone looking to transform the way they work (and play) with others.

DR. JUDY HO, CLINICAL AND FORENSIC NEUROPSYCHOLOGIST, AUTHOR OF *THE NEW RULES OF ATTACHMENT* AND *STOP SELF-SABOTAGE*

In these times of accelerated change and constant disruption, **The "Yes, And" Business Evolution** *provides a beautiful bridge between what is and what can be. Within these pages, the author offers practical, insightful tactics on leveraging the "Yes, And" principles of improv to keep teams moving forward, grounded, and together.*

CHRIS TAYLOR, PRESIDENT & CEO, ACTIONABLE

Having personally experienced the exercises Tracy writes about in her book brought back great memories of fun, laughter-filled, team-building experiences. This book shares table stakes for new leaders and is an excellent reminder of how back-to-basics skills, like listening, can make all the difference in building great teams. Full of practical and easy-to-implement ideas that can develop life skills, enabling outstanding leadership.

NANCY FONSECA, SVP, CLIENT SERVICES,
Great Place To Work® Canada

Drawing from my own journey and knowing the transformative power of the "Yes, And" approach, this book resonated deeply with me. It reminded me that people build bridges of trust when we collaborate and build each other up. This book was full of gems that leaders at all stages can utilize, underscoring the foundational elements of effective communication and collaboration. Tracy brilliantly highlights the often-overlooked essentials, like genuine listening, that pave the way for impactful leadership. This is a guide filled with actionable insights that enhance professional dynamics and enrich our relationships.

DAN SHAIKH, CO-FOUNDER OF SPEAKER SLAM®
AND PUBLICIST FOR INSPIRATIONAL CHANGEMAKERS

Tracy brings connection, communication, and innovation together to create magic! She has decades of experience in both business and improv, and this combination makes her stand out as a heart-centered improv facilitator who can elevate your company's leadership.

RINA ROVINELLI, TOP 25 WOMEN OF INFLUENCE™
CO-FOUNDER OF SPEAKER SLAM® AND SPEAKER COACH

As a college professor for nearly two decades—and a member of the improv theatre community much earlier—I know the power of improv and the "Yes, And" approach. While I initially knew its value on stage, Tracy's book shows the much more important value of "Yes, And" in generating healthier relationships in our daily lives and more productive results in any workplace setting. If you think even a little bit that improv can help you, then say Yes—and read the book. If you think improv is not really for you, then say Yes to accept that there are genuine benefits—and read the book anyway.

MATT AKLER, PROFESSOR, SPORT MANAGEMENT, DURHAM COLLEGE

The definition of leadership is evolving, and so, too, is the way we operate and manage our teams. **The "Yes, And" Business Evolution** *challenges our approach to leadership, using tangible action steps that lead us to a place of connection so all can collectively grow together.*

MIKE SHOREMAN, ATHLETE, SPEAKER, AUTHOR, ADVOCATE

Shea-Porter's vast experience and fresh ideas are clearly conveyed in this high-vibe business book that is equal parts 'how-to' and 'how did we get here?' Essential reading for leaders and team builders who strive for a positive, sustainable workplace.

JUDE KLASSEN, WRITER, DIRECTOR, PRODUCER

THE
"YES, AND"
BUSINESS
EVOLUTION

Improv Skills for Leadership and Life

TRACY SHEA-PORTER

Modern Wisdom Press
Crestone, Colorado, USA

www.modernwisdompress.com

Author photo courtesy of Kathryn Hollinrake Photography.

ISBN: 978-1-7382050-0-4 (paperback), 978-1-7382050-1-1 (epub)

DISCLAIMER

Imagination is more important than knowledge.
Knowledge is limited.
Imagination encircles the world.
—ALBERT EINSTEIN

for Allysha

CONTENTS

FOREWORD

I first met Tracy Shea-Porter back in the mid-'90s. I was working as a program manager for the National Executive MBA Program at the Smith School of Business at Queen's University in Ontario. Tracy was working as marketing communications manager at Bell Canada.

It wasn't Silicon Valley, and we weren't vest-wearing tech bros, yet together, our two organizations completely disrupted higher education. And we did it long before anyone even used the term "disruption."

We delivered an exceptional MBA program from one of Canada's most respected institutions to senior executives in fifteen cities through video conferencing.

You'll notice I didn't say it was through Zoom, Teams, Google Meet, or Webex. No, we used video conferencing, the OG of sound+picture expression. It wasn't through the internet, either. It was through the phone lines. (Yes…phones used to have lines.)

We were the first in North America to do it.

Let me repeat that.

Nobody had done it before.

So, you know what that meant? We had no script to follow. There was no playbook to refer to. No case study had been written. There wasn't a class taught to young business students that explored the HR, financial, marketing, recruiting, pedagogical, and technological implications of beaming an EMBA to a series of small boardrooms across one of the largest countries in the world.

Because of that, there was only one way to do it. We improvised.

We wouldn't have admitted it then, yet we made it all up as we went. We suspended judgment. We thought on our feet. We stretched our comfort zones. We were open to new ideas. We built our confidence, developed trust, and collaborated like never before. Most importantly, we not only listened, we actively listened *and* incorporated what we heard into what we did and said.

It was incredible. And it was all improvised. It had to be.

Most of us start our journeys through life and work with a script written by other people. It's all laid out for us in a clear and logical path to follow, with specific steps to take, milestones to meet, and outputs and destinations to reach.

The weird part? Almost none of us do it.

We face unexpected hardships. We discover new and wonderful experiences. We meet incredible people with unique perspectives. We get opportunities we never dreamed of. We get asked to make both significant and seemingly insignificant choices without any hint of what the result of our decisions will be. We have to veer left when we planned to go right, and we have to zig where others have zagged.

When we look back at it, many of us realize that our proudest moments, our most fulfilling activities, our most rewarding projects, and our best times were when we said, "Yes," even though our heart may have been leaning toward a hard no.

Life *is* improvised. So is work.

And if life and work are improvised, shouldn't we harness our ability, improve our skills, and apply the best approaches of improv so we can be happy, shiny people who have fun, exceed our expectations, accomplish our goals, and lead others so they can achieve theirs?

That was a rhetorical question. Of course we should.

And who better to help us do that than my original partner in innocent crime, Tracy Shea-Porter, otherwise known as TSP.

Tracy and I reconnected years after the Queen's launch, although it wasn't in a classroom or over a video conference. It was in a comedy club. Tracy was exploring and refining all the things that made her successful in business on a stage in a dimly lit room of misfits and rebels. She wasn't launching a program. She was launching a show.

There aren't many outstanding improvisers who truly understand the intricate details of corporate life. Tracy certainly does. There aren't many business people who truly understand the intricate details of improv. Tracy certainly does.

Luckily, you don't have to take an EMBA to benefit from Tracy's experience and expertise. It's right here in your hands. Through these insightful chapters, you'll learn how you can lead with "Yes, And." Cultivate "Yes, And." Build projects, teams, and entire organizations with "Yes, And." And how you can succeed with "Yes, And." In work and life.

3

Where no playbook exists, you now have a playbook. A playbook to suspend judgment. To think on your feet. To stretch your comfort zone. To be open to new ideas. To build your confidence, develop trust, and collaborate like never before—a playbook to listen and incorporate the suggestions and ideas from everyone around you.

Tracy's playbook is your playbook. Go forth and improvise.

—Ron Tite, founder of Church+State
and author of *Everyone's an Artist* and *Think. Do. Say.*

INTRODUCTION

*Play touches and stimulates vitality, awakening the whole person—
mind, body, intelligence and creativity.*

—Viola Spolin

Here you are. You've picked up this book. And you're a leader grappling with a challenge. Perhaps you're part of a leadership team experiencing a communication breakdown. Or your team lacks confidence, or they're bickering. Some people seem to have a need to be right, while other people aren't speaking up. Your stakeholders aren't agreeing about, well, anything. Customers can feel the tension. You're at your wit's end. What to do? You need help. An intervention. Something to help bring effective communication skills to the forefront. Boost creativity. Your company goals are to become agile. Adaptable. Yet, everyone is at odds and there's no clear pathway or direction.

Except there is a way. The "Yes, and" way.

Imagine a world where people listen to each other. They hear one another. They may not agree. That's okay. They cooperate. A world where people stay open to new ideas, as a way to handle conflict. Find common ground. Challenge the egoic concepts of their conditioned minds. Lead with self-awareness—observing themselves and the world around them. A world where people get out of their own heads and into the moment. Confront

5

their own judgments and fears. Invite courage. Empathy. A person says something, and another person adds their point of view to the conversation. There is an agreement to suspend judgment. Acknowledge one another. A world where leaders invite collaboration from other leaders, and team members. Brainstorm. Ideate. In this world, effective communication is a prominent pillar of society. People build bridges of trust. Curiosity and creativity lead the way. There is laughter and play. Imagine.

This is the "Yes, and" way, and you'll learn all about how to create this reality right here within these pages.

In the process of writing this book, however, I encountered a conundrum. I started working on this book in the fall of 2019. Preliminary research—revisiting all the case studies from corporate, education, and government clients who had hired our company, Yes Unlimited, to help their teams collaborate and communicate better. I delved into the improv exercises, role-playing scenarios, and training approaches we'd facilitated to help me focus on best practices and learning outcomes. I knew I had great customer examples, and that I'd done the kind of experiential and creative work with leaders—and teams—that lit me up. I had my why, my sense of purpose, and my reason for showing up to write this book. I was ready.

Throughout almost a decade of operation, our team had connected with thousands of people—in groups of every size—and gathered incredible stories and testimonials about the value of improv in elevating people, teams, and culture. We were ready to share what leaders need to know to be a force of change during this new leadership evolution, to move away from a scarcity, fear-based way of thinking into an open, vulnerable, heart-space way of being. I was moving along, writing a book proposal, collecting examples of our work with leaders that made me smile, and considering the lessons we'd learned along the way.

Then, March 2020 happened. COVID-19. Suddenly, the world was on lockdown, introduced to terms like "social distancing," "flattening the curve," and "home isolation." We were in a pandemic. Everyone. The hashtag #alonetogether emerged. Frontline grocery and healthcare workers became the most important people on the planet—deservedly. And all of the in-person corporate workshops we had booked for Yes Unlimited were canceled—a total necessity. My business partner and Yes Unlimited cofounder, Ralph MacLeod, who also owns and operates the SoCap Comedy Theatre in Toronto (more on him in chapter 1), had to shut down all improv classes and shows. Everything suddenly moved online.

Around the globe, we witnessed the sudden rise of virtual music, theater, and art events. The world needs art, and never more so than during a pandemic, we discovered together. Musicians offered unifying virtual concerts, talk show hosts suddenly became lifelines connecting us to one another by voicing our shared experiences, and people everywhere told stories of their pandemic experiences, forming a collective understanding. The sudden shift was visible in vast and intimate ways. People were singing to one another across balconies, clanging pots and pans all around communities in honor of essential workers. Sharing music and stories and new traditions really helped. Because when people are feeling overwhelmed, connection is even more important. Connection. Perhaps it's everything.

Up until COVID-19, our improv events had been wonderful face-to-face training adventures. Yet once COVID hit, we were faced with a new challenge—thus my conundrum. Could we deliver powerful improv events online? We believed that building online communities could help people and teams connect during COVID too. It wasn't easy, and our progress was slow. We were, after all, dealing with our own very human reactions to the sudden pandemic. Personally, I felt overwhelmed, and my nervous system was on high alert. What was this strange new world, and how might we help? We started by getting together with improvisers and facilitators around the world, collaborating on how to deliver improv—and other team-oriented teachings—online. Authentic, from-the-heart, soul-based experiential exercises to facilitate deep listening, sharing, and relatedness.

What we noticed was interesting: None of our clients responded. Leaders seemed to be working internally—figuring out this strange new world. Finally, I talked with one of my customers— the president of a major software company, to whom we had delivered huge and terrifically received improv events for hundreds of their team members from around the world, the previous two years. These events brought global leaders together, connecting everyone as humans, celebrating their unique backgrounds and histories, teaching each other about where they were from, their languages, and their diverse identities. We created a safe space for people to share little moments in order to build relationships, encourage cooperation, and grow trust: the essential ingredients to strengthen any team and establish strong working partnerships. When I spoke with my customer he said, "We don't need any help, or any improv."

I asked him, "What are you doing?"

He said, "Oh, we're just trying to sell our software."

Selling. Some leaders were on the defensive and worried about profits—this conversation made that clear. Who could blame them? They were scared. Scared of losing their jobs, their incomes, their livelihoods. We human beings tend to go to the fear place when life gets challenging. Our internal "fight-or-flight" response gets activated, and we retreat to our protective spots. Yet, at Yes Unlimited, we believe there is a need for human connection at work at all times. Because putting people first is at the heart of every great workplace. When you lead with heart, support your teammates at all costs, and acknowledge how people are feeling as your first response, you shape your environment into a dynamic space where people want to be.

What shape do you want your environment to be? Do you want people to be afraid? Or nourished? I promise you that if you nourish people, then the profits will arise from a place of gratitude and well-being. Your customers can sense the way your team feels through interaction—and happy employees make happy customers. As a conscious leader, you understand the need to support your team with consistent, ongoing training experiences—learning and development that lets them be heard. You want to help people understand their roles in the larger mission of your organization as well as their immediate tasks. So, while it's true that your company cannot exist without profits, it's also true that your company cannot flourish through all the ups and downs of business life unless your people come first.

After a few more conversations with customers, I decided to pose a question on social media: "I'm working on a piece about communication and work. What words do you associate with work? Curious about what you imagine." A few said "calling," "play," "passion," "career," or "creative party." These words were promising. Yet, the overwhelming number of people thought of work as something negative or something they "had" to do. They offered terms like "hunting/ gathering," "livelihood," "burden," or "labor." I had hoped to make sense of how people were feeling in the context of COVID and how I might help. The responses made me further realize that the world of work is all caught up in negativity, fear, and outdated norms. Something needed to change—and still does. It seemed like the pandemic further highlighted this deep need for transformation.

As Ralph and I talked with more clients, we rolled up our sleeves and went into creativity mode to design virtual improv events. During one such session, I found myself in a virtual breakout room doing an exercise with a woman from California. It was just the two of us. We were to ask one another a simple question. What makes you come alive? She said the ocean. She talked about how much she missed being around people—relating to them or just talking about nothing in particular. She said her daily walks by the ocean were giving her sustenance and helping her get through the pandemic. In response to what she said, according to the prompt we'd designed, I was to offer her a gift. My gift was a special, energy-vibration, pulsating, ocean cloak that she could slip on and off to give her the support, calm, and vitality needed at any time. My turn. What was making me come alive? My response was instantaneous: Writing this book! And her gift was equally heartfelt—she offered me a special, blue, magical energy pen to help me write. I was thrilled. I'd been so immersed in the creative process of imagining this book into being that my answer rang out spontaneously.

Two strangers who had never even met before offered one another helpful support. So, what did we do, and why was it powerful? We listened to one another, we gave one another something personal that would help during those hard times, we were vulnerable, we led with empathy. Playfulness. That was the moment when I knew that yes, true connection *can* be achieved online, and at a distance, and even during a worldwide pandemic. We humans have a fundamental need to connect, and connecting is nonnegotiable if we are to thrive. So, whether your interactions are in person, online, one-on-one, or in a group setting, the principles and power of "Yes, and" connection ring true.

I've enjoyed many similar experiences, in person and online, which prove to me that yes, we can deeply connect, collaborate, and build trust both in person and at a distance. The thing about improv is that it's fun too. You know you're going to laugh. Throughout my years at Yes Unlimited, I have cherished all the little moments of watching people reach that joyful "aha" moment when they experience active listening, or truly give and receive ideas without judgment, while totally present and in-the-moment—laughing together. These moments are what make my heart sing. The bottom line: we truly are all in this together, helping one another thrive. I know that, as a leader, you are deeply interested in helping your team bond and communicate in new ways that break through outdated modes of thinking, opening the door for synergy and creativity to bloom. I know that otherwise, you wouldn't be here, reading this book.

I wrote this book for you. This is a book about how to change your life, your workplace, and indeed the whole world through the power of "Yes, and" communication. It's a book about the power of leading with "Yes, and."

So, what is "Yes, and"? It's the foundational principle of improv. And it is the heart of this book. In the following chapters, we will delve into how improv techniques and the principles of "Yes, and" offer a powerful framework for today's transformational leaders—conscious leaders who are, indeed, also improvisational leaders.

You have in your hands a book about humanity's most innate skill: that intricate dance of giving and receiving known as cooperation. The next step in leadership evolution is upon us. This is a book about improv and the power of "Yes, and" to help leaders and teams elevate their communication and creativity skills. And, it's a book about how leading with "Yes, and" will change your life as a person, whether you're a leader or team member. After all, we're all the leaders of our own lives.

As I write this, it's 2023, and leaders everywhere are adapting to a hybrid location model—with people working both at home and in the office. Communicating clearly with team members and stakeholders has never been more important. Helping employees tell their stories, speak up, listen to one another, and connect all continue to be at the forefront of work. Employee engagement through recognition—a focus on well-being, diversity, flexibility, and, yes, inspiring people—is needed more than ever. People need to feel cared about and encouraged. They need to have opportunities for growth. How can you help? By leading with heart. This is where improv comes in—restoring balance through the art of "Yes, and."

The place is here and the time is now. Let's "Yes, and" this!

CHAPTER ONE

Leading with "Yes, And"

I define connection as the energy that exists between people when they feel seen, heard, and valued; when they can give and receive without judgment; and when they derive sustenance and strength from the relationship.

—BRENÉ BROWN

Toxic Leadership

It's 1988, and I'm a twenty-something customer relations professional working at a midsize technology company in Toronto. The owner—I'll call him Rodney—has banned all women in the office from ever wearing pants. The receptionist, a highly efficient and intelligent young woman whom I'll call Elsa, is defiant. She wants to be comfortable. She also has a health condition, which means that comfort is super important to her. Rodney tells Elsa that he is going to fire her for wearing pants. And he does. The next day, I arrive at the office to find that Elsa has indeed been fired. We're all outraged. And yet, when Elsa was fired, nobody did anything. Rodney did what he wanted and made all the rules. Everyone was scared.

You could say that Rodney exerted "power over," a phrase that Brené Brown describes in her book *Dare to Lead* as "using fear to protect and hoard power" (Brown 2018). This kind of thinking is all about a need to be right, to wield control. There was no collaboration between employees. No conversation about office protocol. It was Rodney's way or the highway. I took the highway and quit that job shortly after, yet I never forgot the lesson—if you are working in a company where the leader has all the say and doesn't listen, you can give in, get out, or try for a breakthrough. These choices were presented to me at different times throughout my career, and I tried to make my decision based on courage over fear. At that time and place, "get out" was the way for me, and it led me on this journey to you now, where I can share this story as a case study in poor leadership—and open the door for a new conversation about how to effect change.

It's 1999. I'm a communications manager at a large software company as part of a team of marketing professionals. Our new boss, whom I will call Louise, is meeting with us about a recent strategic company plan, which has been totally created by senior management, with no input from the team that will actually execute the tactics. As she presents the document, and tells us what we'll be doing, faces around the table appear crestfallen, and defeated, with eyes cast downward. Without "reading the room" Louise cheerily continues presenting the plan, without engaging in a back-and-forth dialogue, asking for input, or inviting questions. Someone raises their hand—and Louise says, "Not now," in a dismissive tone, and continues to speak without listening. From the body language in evidence during the meeting and the conversations that erupted later, it was clear that the team felt disrespected and demotivated.

It's 2023. I've been a business owner since 2007, and I'm a trusted improvisation trainer and sales and marketing consultant for a wide range of national and international companies. During an introduction meeting with a new client, I learn that the senior management team is continuously rotating through the company as if through a revolving door. The latest senior manager I'm working with is a toxic man. He shouts out his expectations in meetings, belittling his team. His approach creates conflict and problems. I learn that every salesperson on his team has complained. One year into his tenure, this man continues to treat his team with disdain, humiliating everyone and making them feel small and anxious. People have quit. Eventually, this man is fired, though not before creating widespread havoc that negatively impacts performance and profits.

What year is this in your career as you read these examples? How are things going in your working world? Throughout my thirty-five-year-long corporate career, I've worked with all kinds of leaders—some fantastic, some not so much. As you read these stories, do examples of toxic leadership come to mind for you? Have you experienced "power over" scenarios with the people you've reported to at work? It's interesting to note that many people are in positions of power who have no business overseeing people. Yet this is absolutely nothing new. Some call it "the old boys' network." Yet, harmful leadership styles are not exclusive to men. I've seen good and bad leaders of all kinds through the years. I could fill books with examples of dangerous leadership styles I've witnessed throughout my career, as I worked with companies ranging from telecommunications to government to software companies, and everything in between. And worse, I've seen leaders target people—break them down—and fire them for absolutely no good reason. (You can't wear pants? I mean, come on!)

I'm going to go out on a limb here and say that in every case—including in every case of the toxic leadership I've described (or that you've experienced)—it's not entirely the leader's fault. I know. Sounds ridiculous. Absurd. How can I say that? The answer is that all those harmful, noxious, pernicious leaders are operating from an internal code called "conditioning," which tells them to do, talk, and act in particular ways. What is conditioning? Well, learned patterns, behaviors, and beliefs. We all have them, and we all need to keep an eye on what we've been taught, because frequently nobody tells unhealthy leaders to stop—and that's old, outdated conditioning too. Today's problematic leaders have learned malignant approaches from other bad leaders and so on and so on. It's multigenerational bad leadership. An abundance of exaggerated ego.

There Is Another Way

There are definitely great leaders in the world who can effectively show us the way forward. You know them. They're the ones who take the time to listen to you, and really hear what you are saying. They acknowledge people and aren't afraid to share the spotlight. When they make mistakes, they own up—and demonstrate how making mistakes is an opportunity for growth and learning. They don't need to adopt "power over" because they're more interested in building a great team, helping people rise up, and motivating those around them to improve and contribute. They have vision and are open to new ideas—creativity and innovation. Great leaders inspire. They're frequently humble. Could it be that they naturally grew to be that way, based on their own internal codes and conditioning? In the big picture, many organizations have been progressing toward more effective leadership (slowly) through the improved company policies and procedures that have been adopted after decades of workplace challenges. There has been a rise in training as well, aiming to shift some of the worn-out power patterns that need to go. Yet, we need more innovative learning and development programs. It's not enough to put forth a set of rules and expect everyone to simply follow them, or else. Having a variety of different styles of training to suit different types of team members will help people gain the self-awareness techniques needed to manage well in a complex world.

What's also missing is a simple, easy-to-remember communication tool that we can all learn from. Something we can say to one another that gives permission for leaders to talk with other leaders and teams, inviting everyone to collaborate in a new way. Something that encourages people to communicate with one another in a way that builds authentic trust. A way of being that gets away from this "I am right" notion and leads with a humility, sharing, and common ground that invites respect.

I propose "Yes, and."

What Is "Yes, And"?

At the heart of improv is the foundational principle of "Yes, and."

In simple terms, the "Yes" part means *I am listening*, while the "and" part means *I am speaking up*. We are having a conversation. We offer one another respect while we communicate, even if we don't agree on the topic. (It's important to know that "Yes, and" does not mean you have to agree—it simply means you are hearing and suspending judgment while you listen.) While you are "Yes-ing" (listening), I am "and-ing" (speaking). We are listening and speaking. Giving and receiving. Staying open to each other's ideas. This powerful communication tool allows for affirmation and collaboration.

It's a way to communicate that says yes, I'm hearing you. I'll listen to you, and then I'll have a turn, and you'll listen to me. We'll agree to that. And, from there, as we exchange ideas back and forth, perhaps something new will arise. A new idea we couldn't even imagine without agreeing to have this conversation. "Yes, and" is ultimately about building trust and mutual understanding. When we listen to one another, we open a pathway. We may be changed by one another. We may grow. Evolve. Inspire one another.

Yes = Listening (I Receive)

- Accepting

- Acknowledging

- Hearing

And = Speaking Up (I Give)

- Building

- Connecting

- Inspiring

One person is "Yes-ing" (listening) while another person is "and-ing" (speaking). The person speaking makes an offer, and the person listening will soon "and" by adding their idea to the initial offer. Through this cooperative back-and-forth exchange, we stay open to new ideas, even if we don't agree, and we resolve to hear one another. Perhaps a new understanding, or idea, will arise through this simple yet profound improv practice.

Why Not Get Experiential Right Now?

Let's do a quick "Yes, and" exercise together right now. This is a book about improv after all, and perhaps the best way to grasp "Yes, and" is to take it out of the abstract and actually do it.

You don't need anyone else to do this exercise. We'll make a salad together. First, I will add an ingredient, and then you will add an ingredient, and at the end, we'll have the makings of a dish. Just read my ingredient and then add your ingredient as we experience "Yes, anding" one another.

Me: For our salad together, I would like to add kale.

You: "Yes, and" I would like to add (fill in the blank).

Me: "Yes, and" I would like to add red peppers.

You: "Yes, and" I would like to add (blank).

Me: "Yes, and" I would like to add pumpkin seeds.

You: "Yes, and" I would like to add (blank).

Me: "Yes, and" I would like to add sunshine.

You: "Yes, and" I would like to add (blank).

End Scene!

How was that? Did you get a feel for what "Yes, and" is all about? In a lot of ways, the experiential nature of "Yes, and" needs to be engaged with through the experience of doing. One of my top priorities in writing this book is to encourage you to start using the words "Yes, and" or the phrase "Let's 'Yes, and' this," in your daily communication. Speak them out loud when adding your point to a conversation. Speak them internally when clarifying an idea to yourself. "Yes, and" yourself. "Yes, and" your family, friends, and colleagues. Open up to the beauty and grace of staying open to the ideas of other people while also honoring your own ideas.

What you will notice is that my offerings of kale, red peppers, and pumpkin seeds created a response in you. And, your response is totally based on every experience you've ever had with kale, red peppers, and pumpkin seeds. You see, whether you love or hate those ingredients is entirely based on your personal views. Another way of saying it is that your collection of stories and thoughts (your unique ego) creates a response every time. And the response will be different for everyone.

I threw in a surprise at the end—the sun. Perhaps you smiled, or maybe you laughed, or grimaced—every response is a good response. Because it's your response. Your unique addition to our scene together. If we had a group together and were adding different ingredients, all kinds of ideas would emerge—we would start with food and other items would be added like a table, a chair, or a cat. Really, it's limitless. The more people you get together to discuss anything, the more ideas emerge. And nobody would agree on everything. You don't have to agree. Not at all. You might hate red peppers. Or, maybe you're getting hungry. Personally, I'm making a salad right now.

The point is we want to stay open and listen to each other. Really listen. That's the crux. You see, we're often thinking about our own response instead of listening—tuning out, or off in another land. Whether you agree or not, the aim is to listen and build on what the other person is saying (and vice versa). You will find that, out of this collaboration of ideas, something new emerges. That's the beauty of "Yes, and"—to let us create something new, stay open, and stop the judge in our brain. (There is a more detailed "Yes, and" exercise in chapter 7, so stay tuned for a deep dive into this helpful communication tool.)

> "To me 'Yes, and' means don't be afraid to contribute. It's your responsibility to contribute. Always make sure you're adding something to the discussion. Your initiations are worthwhile."
>
> —Tina Fey

Improv Supports Self-Awareness and Openness Through "Yes, And"

Our simple salad exchange is a straightforward yet effective way to create some initial awareness and space within you and help you open up to new ways of learning. The next step is observing. Now, making a salad is a fairly easy example, since we can agree to disagree on certain foods—and we can agree to eat only our own food selections, if we want. We want to exercise this improv muscle to train up our brain (opening to new ideas—giving and receiving—Yes, and–ing). We can create a place in our psyche to say, "Yes, I am listening to you. I am hearing you. Your voice is important." Now, we are sharing information and also adding new ideas and experiences to our lives in the moment. If improv does one thing in a most excellent way, it creates presence. You cannot be anywhere else except in the moment when you are doing improv. This is where the magic happens. This is where the transformation begins. Now. Right here. Let's "Yes, and" this.

You will notice that when you start saying "Yes, and" (instead of "No" or "But," for example), there is a positive energy and flow that emerges in your conversations. Whether you are having a conversation with yourself, a neighbor, or a colleague or at the grocery store, "Yes, and" creates a confident, dynamic momentum. Moreover, this "Yes, and–ing" expands into all areas of your life and has a compounding effect, inviting a kind of receptiveness to the world inside and around you. I've felt it and I've witnessed it for years. And since our working lives involve a great deal of our time and energy, and because many of us experience stress and pressure through our careers, doesn't it make sense to extend that transformative experience to our professional lives? Let's look at how that can be done.

Improv at Work

When we first start working with leaders and teams, we ask them what they think about improv. Words like "comedy," "funny," "humor," "standup," and "sketch" rise to the surface. Groups like Monty Python and Second City and shows like *Whose Line Is It Anyway?* and *Saturday Night Live* are named. *Improv* and *funny* are fused together in the collective consciousness. With good reason. Improv is playful. And you will laugh. Yet people think they have to be innately funny, good at speaking in public, and super quick on the spot. In other words, comedy performers. This means improv is scary to a lot of people. The truth is people just need to be themselves. And showing up as our authentic selves can also be scary at times. We put people at ease by creating a safe space for stretching comfort zones and getting comfortable with trying something new. And, it's fun. Pretty soon, everyone is laughing and having a great time.

As improvisers, we learned a set of techniques, rules, and methods to help us build scenes on the spot. Turns out these techniques are highly transferable to helping build harmonious and productive teams. The reason: it's all about learning how to communicate effectively while boosting creativity.

Improv for business is actually nothing new. Bringing improv exercises into corporate life has been going on for decades, with terrific results. That's why improv for business continues to grow. It's part of our evolution. History shows that the Atellan Farces of Italy, which started around 300 BCE, were early works of improv art. The foundational principle of improv—the "Yes, and" philosophy—was codified in the 1950s by Viola Spolin, an American theater educator, widely regarded as the mother of improvisational theater (Spolin 2003). This "Yes, and" acceptance principle, which informs most improv exercises, is now also used to develop nonperformance skills like team building, "thinking on your feet," collaboration, creativity, and all-around effective communication, to name a few. This nonperformance evolution of improv also has a name: Applied Improvisation.

Applied Improvisation

The term Applied Improvisation surfaced in the late 1990s as a way to "apply" improv methods to nontheatrical fields. The techniques that help comedy teams create great sketches can be "applied" to other scenarios, like corporate training. This field has really taken off around the world. So, when Applied Improvisation facilitators get together with leaders and teams, they aren't teaching them to be performers—not at all. They're customizing certain improv exercises to support business objectives. These objectives are far-ranging. Improv training can be customized to help a team bond, develop confidence and active listening skills, or teach coworkers how to brainstorm and solve company challenges together. Experiential improv exercises develop presentation, storytelling, sales, networking, public speaking, and overall communication and creativity skills. Improv is also all about expanding your comfort zone and embracing failure—while you laugh! That's a key point of improv. You let go of perfection and give in to the spontaneous moment.

With improv, mistakes are where the magic happens. In fact, every blunder creates an opportunity for transformation. Improv teaches us that not only is failure okay, it's necessary for growth and often the stepping stone to improvement. We need to reimagine the concept of failure in the business world as an opportunity, rather than something to be feared. When people are afraid at work, they don't say anything, they stop participating, and they shut down. Improv supports the creation of a synergistic, collaborative environment.

Improv is a team skill. And, since improv techniques are highly transferable to teams at work, they support learning and development. It's not really a surprise. After all, improv is all about having each other's back, vulnerability, empathy, showing up, and, of course, that all-important foundational pillar "Yes, and." At the heart of "Yes, and" is effective communication. And at the heart of teamwork? Working together toward a common goal. To be a cohesive team means listening to, supporting, and trusting one another. That's having each other's back. "Yes, and" creates the framework for effective collaboration. Creativity and innovation flourish. "Yes, and" means I acknowledge what you are saying, I am listening to your idea (again, even if we don't agree), and I am adding my idea to your idea. "Yes, and" transforms communication through the respectful sharing of ideas. "Yes, and" creates positive momentum toward empowerment—in ourselves and in other people.

How Can Improv and "Yes, And" Help You and Your Team Communicate Better?

Let us count the ways.

Throughout this book, we are going to dig into how the shift in perspective that comes from improv can enhance your communications, creativity, and life. Since this is a book written for businesses, we will focus on how improv can concretely support leaders and teams, enhance your collaboration, and nourish your corporate culture. We will also touch on ways improv can augment social skills, mindfulness, and well-being, since how you show up in your life supports how you show up at work—everything's connected. Overall, the emphasis is on how improv helps leaders and teams develop effective communication and creativity skills.

Throughout the thousands of conversations I've had with business leaders, common themes emerge. In many cases, leaders want to help their teams open up, speak up, gain courage to talk openly in meetings, and quite simply, build connection.

In fact, team building is the number one request we receive when creating an improv training experience. Sometimes, though, leaders think of themselves as separate from their team, as though the team needs "help" and they are an outside entity. Actually, it's important that leaders take part in the training too. Team bonding means the whole team—and that includes the leader. This disconnection is part of the challenge, as leaders may not see their own blind spots, their own areas in need of improvement.

Remember my leadership examples at the start of this chapter? Those leaders lacked self-awareness, and based on their behaviors, they also lacked good training. Sure, sometimes we create separate events for leaders and teams—when the focus is different. Yet overall, the point is that everyone gets in on the training. Ideally, a series of improv events will help build trust between different groups over time and will expand on important company themes, inviting everyone to participate together at certain points.

We're all working on something, whether large or small, and learning and development is an ongoing practice that everyone needs to experience.

Often, new learning involves unlearning old perceptions and habits in order to adopt new ways of being and seeing the world. So, when you are helping your team develop presentation skills, sales skills, and their own leadership skills—confidence—you want to lead with a supportive attitude. It's vital that you are part of the shift, that you are in the process of learning too. (Notice I keep mentioning the word "skills"—that's because improv is a team skill and it's also an individual and leadership skill). We talk about building trust. Having each other's back. How to overcome fear of failure (that's a big one). It comes down to creating an environment where people understand that it's okay to share. Their ideas won't be dismissed. A place where leading with "Yes, and" is recognized and valued.

Here are a few client scenarios that we've worked with over the years. Do you see you and your team here?

The **chief executive officer** of a midsize national shipping company sought help with company morale, as prior management had taught people their ideas were not worthy. The team felt negative, shut down, and isolated. The result of improv training was to help create a new culture where people felt supported to come forward with ideas, confident that they would be listened to and that everyone "had each other's back."

The **sales director** of a large, international luxury fashion house wanted their customer-facing sales teams to bring storytelling skills, active listening, respect, and gratitude to their customer engagement experience. A focus on combining improv and role-playing helped the team loosen up and open themselves to inspired training with real-world scenarios, which positively impacted customer interaction and resulted in stronger profits.

The **director** of a national start-up company wanted to encourage fun, laughter, and connection to help the team remain agile and adaptable through stressful, high-demand times, and to support a collaborative environment. The outcome was team bonding through "Yes, and" interactions, with a secondary focus on "thinking on your feet" skills to help people stay present in the moment, build trust, and respond to challenges through active listening and curiosity.

The **finance director** at a large multinational bank wanted to encourage bold candor, positive disruption, improved stakeholder relations, and multiteam collaboration. The plan was to employ experiential improv exercises focused on authentic voice, impromptu presentation and storytelling skills, and "Yes, and" conversations to enhance overall effective communication skills.

The **Career Center director** of a large national university wanted to help students overcome anxiety and learn workplace communication skills, networking, and overall confidence boosting. The outcome was to create an environment of connection, where the students learned to access their authentic voice through verbal and nonverbal techniques, as well as presence and laughter, leading to enhanced courage-building and self-assurance.

When you adopt an improvisational environment, you will notice improved:

Trust. Confidence. Team bonding. Connection.
Collaboration. Innovation. "Thinking on your feet."
Curiosity. Active listening. Courage. Storytelling.
Authentic voice. Agility. Adaptability. Speaking up.
Brainstorming. Empathy. Presence. "Yes, and." Gratitude.

All of these words amount to the same goal: A need to develop personal skills that support interpersonal environments. In a word, communication. By developing a framework for personal development, and effective communication, you can then encourage greater creativity—as an individual, a leader, and a team member. And what's stopping people from communicating more effectively? In a word, fear. Fear of failure. Fear of being seen as "less than." Fear of being ridiculed and rejected. Sometimes, structure is the culprit. The hierarchical organization of companies contributes to a toxic environment where people are afraid to speak up. This focus on rigid status within organizations results in people shutting down and disengaging. Other times, leaders and teams have no clear direction and training on how to build a cooperative exchange of ideas together.

Why wouldn't people feel fear? It's built in. It's how our brains keep us safe. How we evolved as humans. You know—fight, flight, freeze, fawn, flop. Even though we aren't being chased by saber-toothed cats anymore (well, not most of us, and not all of the time), we are often on high alert for something terrible to happen. Like when an email we didn't mean to send gets unleashed to the world. We're wired that way. Problem is, staying steadily on high alert increases our cortisol (you know, that stress hormone that is helpful during real times of distress, and can be less helpful if we get too much too often). We need to find ways to stay relaxed, open—to feel good—and to invite those lovely dopamine, oxytocin, and serotonin endorphins into our daily world. That's why appreciation for meditation, yoga, nature walks, breathing exercises, and overall mindfulness is on the rise. Our hustling, over-the-top way of living has us stressed out and spaced out. And when that happens, we often stop doing anything at all. We're stuck. So, if you are a leader who thinks paying attention to your team's well-being is an expendable "soft skill," think again. A stressed-out team is an unproductive team, and that affects your bottom line. So, attention to your team's well-being and skills development doesn't just make you a good human—it also supports your company's profits.

THE SAD STATE OF EMPLOYEE ENGAGEMENT

A 2019 global study by the ADP Research Institute (across 19 countries with 1,000 respondents in each country) shows that only about 16 percent of employees are engaged at work, while about 84 percent are going through the motions. What does this mean? When employees are not engaged—are not invested in the company's goals and values—they are tuned out, unproductive, and disconnected. And ineffective people impact your bottom line.

What do employees need? Connection, an environment where "you have each other's back," a sense of purpose, and consistent, ongoing support to feel like they are part of a team that cares. (Buckingham and Goodall 2019).

Engagement Matters

When employees feel engaged, they adopt the vision, values, and purpose of your company. You can anticipate that people will become lively contributors, inventive problem solvers, and synergistic colleagues. When you see a team member—or even an entire team—appear indifferent, passive, and disengaged, it really points to a bigger problem. Typically, the challenge is one of leadership. Ask yourself, how do you appear at work? How about the leadership team overall? Are you engaged? How clear are you on your goals and expectations? Is the company mission clearly expressed? Are you supportive? It all adds up to company culture. We humans need to feel a sense of belonging and want to be striving for a higher purpose. What meaning can we apply to our working day?

This focus on clarity around personal and professional values is truly important. We need to have regular conversations about how our professional and personal lives can intertwine effectively. And guess what? It all starts with leadership. How you appear as an individual, team, and company leader offers a beacon of light showing the way. How do you show up?

Breaking Through Our Fear-Armor

When we first start improv training with people, we want to help everyone feel at ease and gain a sense of comfort so they can relax. At the beginning of each session, people are always a little hesitant. We notice this sense of reserve through body language, for example. Folded arms. A shy glance. Nervous laughter. A skittish tone. The point is to get to a place of individual and group confidence.

In her 2018 book *Dare to Lead*, acclaimed research professor Brené Brown calls it "grounded confidence." She says, "It's not fear that gets in the way of courage, it's armor—how we self-protect when we feel uncertain or fearful." How do we chisel through our own armor? It's about showing up. Showing up for ourselves and other people. When we show up—break through our fear-armor—we expand ourselves. We open to possibilities. Brown suggests that we "rumble with vulnerability, stay curious, and practice new skills." I agree. Improv gets us there. Through improv, we walk alongside one another as we stretch our comfort zones. Suddenly we're laughing together, bonding in new ways, and exploring a new team dynamic. Our armor slips away. We've created something new together. Creating "grounded confidence" with your colleagues is a crucial step in growing an engaged team. You all need to understand that you're there for each other. That's when you invite permission to get creative and innovative. It all starts with building a foundation of trust.

A Word About "No"

When we're talking about "Yes, and," people always ask about "No." Isn't "No" an important word too? Yes, it is. "No" is an important and powerful word. Necessary and useful—at the right moments. "No" is all about stopping, shutting things down, and blocking what's happening. Sometimes saying no is absolutely essential. "No" is reflected in the stop sign that helps traffic flow smoothly; the boundaries we set to honor our personal time, space, and needs; and "No means no" when we aren't giving our consent in a certain situation. Communicating with "No!" has a vital place in our lives.

At the same time, the word "No" can also be used to control, evade, and appear to be right. In leadership—building strong, resilient, effective teams and collaborative communication—how we apply "Yes, and" or "No" becomes crucial. "No" is not a great word when you are inviting teams to open up, share ideas, and listen to one another. When it comes to personal development, leadership, and creating strong, vibrant teams, we need more "Yes." "Yes" has an energetic quality that encourages risk-taking, offers an open-hearted approach to life and vulnerability, and encourages deep listening. Moreover, it's half of the foundational principle of improv—which says "Let's 'Yes, and' this conversation."

RESEARCH SHOWS:
THE WORD "NO" CAN EVEN BE "DANGEROUS"

The word "No" can even be "dangerous," as reported in a 2012 *Psychology Today* article. Studies show the word "No," heard over and over, floods our bodies with stress-producing hormones and neurotransmitters. When we are in situations where we can expect to hear "No" often, we feel angry, we shut down, and our ability to communicate is stifled. In contrast, studies show that "Yes" contributes to well-being, positivity, and improved health (Newberg and Waldman 2012). The article goes on to say that if you want your life to flourish, you'll need to express at least five positive messages for every negative one. Positivity impacts the motivational centers in the brain and supports resilience.

Your *Yes, And* Book Journey

This book gives you an introduction to how you and your team can learn to communicate better through the practice of improv. And improv is a practice—like yoga, music, and sports. Like life. Notice how I mention yoga, an individual practice, and also music and sports, which both often require team skills. The truth is that everything is always an individual practice too. Just as you practice a yoga pose, your musical instrument, or your physical sports abilities, learning how to communicate well is both an individual and a team skill. That's why I talk about both individual and team exercises in these pages. The exercises are meant to offer a taste test, or experiential introduction, to improv exercises. This book is not meant to be a "train the trainers" guide, although there are basic exercises in these pages for you to try on your own, or with a partner. Really, it's all about offering an exploratory view—a high-level look—at how improv can meaningfully uplevel your leadership and life.

Along with this discussion of the profound power of "Yes, and," case studies and personal stories are sprinkled throughout the chapters. Expect to read more about my own experiences as I brought improv principals into the workplace, first as a young communications professional, then as a team leader, and finally as an entrepreneur leading my own experiential improv training company, Yes Unlimited, with a particular focus on business and education through the lens of Applied Improvisation. And finally, in the appendix, you'll have a chance to review some improv exercises as I share real-world examples of our own experiences with teams. Again, the exercises offer a review, and are not presented in a format for training. They're meant to spark your imagination, and inspire you to invite improv facilitation into your world.

As I noted earlier, the tools described in this book are the product of a collaboration, and this is a good moment to introduce my business partner, Ralph MacLeod, to you. Ralph is a world-class improv teacher and facilitator, and he owns the SoCap Comedy Theatre in Toronto. Ralph and I met in Toronto's improv community somewhere in the mid- to late '90s. About a decade ago, he approached me to engage on the corporate improv side of things for his theater, and the rest is history. We created Yes Unlimited out of a passion for improv.

Ralph figures throughout this book because not only do we often facilitate together, we also co-own our company Yes Unlimited. Funny story. When we were thinking up company names, Ralph had a dream. Like an actual dream—the sleeping kind. In this dream the name Yes Unlimited popped up. We like to think it was divine intervention. Kinda like how we want "Yes, and" to be an unlimited way for people to communicate. Our dream is that "Yes, and" is embraced around the world as a way to listen, really hear another person, build on their idea with your own whether you agree or not, find common ground, dig deep, and resolve conflicts. That's just for starters. So, the dreams (sleeping kind and waking kind) merged, and here we are.

More than anything, this is a kind of love song to the power of human connection through play. And it is my heartfelt offering to you, as you deepen your humanity by cultivating improv and "Yes, and" philosophies in your practice as a leader.

What to Expect as You Read and Explore This Book

These chapters can be read as standalone, as well as in order, and you may want to take your time with them. You'll definitely find some repetition, such as a conversation about the importance of active listening, interwoven throughout each chapter. Learning through repetition is a key improv skill. You want to disrupt old behaviors, and that means spotlighting new learnings.

- Chapter 1, this one here, introduces you to the foundational principle of improv, "Yes, and," and sets the stage for what's to come.

- In chapter 2, we'll explore why improv is an important training tool for companies to adopt and how "Yes, and" thinking can facilitate deep change.

- Then, in chapter 3, we deep dive into the "Yes, and" team. Building trust through playfulness. Making room for creativity and innovation to flourish. Helping confidence grow. Creating adaptive teams where people are supported and encouraged.

- Chapter 4 delves into the new conscious leader (that's you). It makes the case that a leader who guides their team with a "we" instead of a "me" mentality is also an improvisational leader.

- In chapter 5, we explore the "Yes, and" individual (you again) and the whys and hows of an individual practice that supports who you are as a leader.

- The focus of chapter 6 is on how to be a "Yes, and" leader. This chapter offers a folio of improv strategies for workplaces, helping leaders build the skills that can help them deeply connect to their teams.

- In chapter 7, we focus on the "Yes, and" company evolution, as well as how conscious, improvisational leaders also create conscious, improvisational companies, leading to adaptable and agile company cultures.

One Last Thing: A Word About Words

Throughout these pages, I'll be applying a vocabulary particular to the field of improv, as well as language specific to linking improv to professional situations. If you want to review certain words and phrases, I encourage you to explore the glossary at the end of the book.

Sound Good?

I am so excited to take you on this journey with me—delving into practices, case studies, experiential teachings, and learnings—to guide you on your "Yes, and" voyage. And the travels never end because—like all practices—we deepen our relationship with ourselves and other people as we go. So, let's begin, shall we?

Chapter Summary

- "Yes, and" is the foundational principle of improv.
- "Yes, and" does not necessarily mean you agree with another person—you take turns listening and speaking while staying open, building on each other's ideas.

- A key aspect of "Yes, and" is deep active listening— hearing one another with the intention of truly listening, rather than listening to respond.

- Applied Improvisation is the term to describe nonperformance improv training techniques that can be "applied" to other scenarios, like corporate training.

- "No" is also important. We want to use the word "No" in certain situations, like when creating boundaries, or when we need to stop or shut down a conversation or event. However, the word "No" can also be a barrier to open communication between leaders and teams.

- Improv exercises and "Yes, and" communication develop powerful business skills and are an important part of leadership and development training programs.

CHAPTER TWO

Conducting the
"Yes, And" Experiment

*There are people who prefer to say "yes" and there
are people who prefer to say "no." Those who say
"yes" are rewarded by the adventures they have.
Those who say "no" are rewarded by the safety
they attain.*

—Keith Johnstone

It's 1987, and I'm walking along Yonge Street, near Eglinton,
in Toronto. I'm embarking on a career in corporate
communications, and I'm thinking about shoulder pads. They're
all the rage in women's fashion, and I'm wondering, *Should
I be wearing shoulder pads?* Will shoulder pads make me appear
more powerful, more masculine? (A common female desire
in the 1980s, when it came to the working world—a fashion
statement meant to help women blend "shoulder to shoulder"
with men). Will I be taken more seriously as a young twenty-
something professional? I feel confused and bewildered as
I attempt to navigate this complex business world. I walk
into the media and publishing offices, where I am employed
as a public relations event coordinator and copywriter. I start
typing copy on my IBM Selectric typewriter, hop on my rotary
phone to make some quick calls, and prepare to fax my copy for
approvals. Shoulder pads. Shoulder pads. What to do?

The night before, I'd attended my first improv show. Something called Theatresports at Harbourfront. There was an intoxicating energy about improv that drew me in. Laughing with gleeful abandon created a kind of euphoria. (I didn't yet know about the power of laughter to release that feel-good empathy hormone oxytocin or how laughter helps bond people together.) I planned to go back and attend a class. At lunch, I swing by a clothing store and try on some jackets with shoulder pads. Power dressing, it is called. They feel kind of funny—like a costume. I go back to the office and type some copy for an in-store magazine promotion and plan a special advertisers' event for the launch of a new brand.

Shoulder pads. Improv. Copywriting. Event planning. A swirl of activity and learning as my early-career-woman self was getting her start. This was a time when women were figuring out who they wanted to be at work. And there were few tools to teach you how to communicate at the office, collaborate as a team, or build trust. Training? I don't recall many workplace learning and development programs during this time. The main idea that was presented to us was to separate our careers from our private lives and leave all that messy human stuff at home. (That didn't happen, I noticed.) Everyone smoked cigarettes in the office too. Imagine that. "Excuse me, Tracy"—*puff, puff,* goes the senior sales manager—"can you fax this document?"

The next week, I went back to Harbourfront, where I didn't just attend a show. I was so enthralled by this fun, exciting community that I also joined an improv class, so I could actually learn how to improvise. What I didn't know yet was that the skills I was about to learn in improv were highly transferable to the rapidly evolving corporate world. And that, as I would become involved at a deep experiential level as the working world changed, I would bring improv skills to my day-to-day life, including my working life. I didn't recognize this for a long time. Yet, I said "Yes" to improv, simply because it felt right and my intuition led me there. This is how it started. A professional woman starting a career alongside a new hobby, learning "on my feet" as I traveled new paths. And that has made all the difference.

What have you said yes to that you didn't totally get at the time—yet, looking back, you can see how that "Yes" played a significant role in your life? What can you say "Yes" to now?

Flash Forward

It's 2019. I have my own company now, and I'm conducting improv training sessions with the sales team of a high-end, international luxury fashion and cosmetics house. We've worked with this company before—they came to Ralph's theater to learn the art of improv and help their sales teams open up to new ways to communicate with customers. Their leadership team has asked us to engage with them on a series of in-depth, full-day improv and role-playing sessions to help their team of thirty in-store salespeople learn more about storytelling skills. Empathy. Active listening. Vulnerability. This day is all about increasing their confidence, helping them find their authentic inner story flow and voice. This is my second day of training with the team alone. On the first day, we started the way most improv sessions start—everyone on their feet in a circle, engaging in dynamic, interactive exercises designed to create new ways of being at work.

On that second day, as usual, I start with breathing exercises to help everyone relax and focus. Then, I throw something new into the mix. I have everyone spread their arms straight out from their sides and say, "I'm grateful." And I talk about how the brain responds to playfulness and gratitude as a great way to start the day. (Back to the beautiful impacts of play as a way to access those all-important natural chemicals of dopamine and serotonin.) I talk about how we can change our state immediately by expressing gratitude, making us feel better, as an important daily practice. You could say gratitude is the balm for the soul—and an active ingredient for transformation. We continue on and have a great day of improv, role-playing, and interactive playfulness.

Well, the next day, as I approach the group, everyone automatically creates a circle. It moves me to see everyone bonding with each other through the practice of improv. They are smiling, happy, and joyful. Once again, we start with breathwork—the great enhancer of mental clarity. Suddenly, without prompting, everyone spreads their arms wide and starts chanting "I'm grateful" with faces showing so much elation, wonder, and something else—I see relief. People appear to be relieved that they are allowed to feel the sensation of gratitude at work. They have permission to simply be. *Why are people feeling relieved?* I wonder.

I pondered this question for a while, and over time, as I observed more and more groups interacting, I arrived at some insights. People need to focus on their breath, experience gratitude, and experience play on a regular basis. All the time. Not only after they leave the office, on special occasions, or at some future holiday gathering. These feelings of gratitude and connection can be layered on top of whatever activity is happening in the moment. Whether you are typing away on a computer, in a meeting, collaborating with a colleague, or brainstorming your next project, this feeling of joy is a necessary part of being human.

Somewhere along the way, joy and work became polar opposites. Work has often been associated with drudgery and dread (back to that little social media poll in the Introduction). An anecdote comes to mind: About six months later, I was at a restaurant, and while I didn't realize it, members of that team were at the table next to me. A number of them came up and approached me to say, "We just had to say hi and thank you." Their words were a great reminder of how experiential events deeply impact people in a powerful way. They remembered the experience because something clicked. They felt the power of experiential improv—wholly connected in the present moment to their gratitude and sense of play—and they experienced this connection at a deeper level, something that stays with a person and expands what their idea of work can be. It didn't hurt that this training had also been spectacularly successful. The director of training had informed me that all our objectives had been met—incorporating a fun, dynamic, animated, and less inhibited approach to sales—creating a client experience for customers, rather than simply a sales approach. The results positively impacted their monthly sales goals too. I strongly believe that the enjoyment of the experience for the team equated to a successful outcome for the leaders. People embody the experiential in ways that translate beautifully to real-world situations.

A Workplace Evolution in the Works

So, what's happened since 1987?

One thing we know for sure: Technology changed. A lot. Typewriter to computer. Fax machine to . . . computer. Rotary phone to cell phone. And shoulder pads to . . . casual business wear. (Okay, there have been a lot of fashion changes—who can keep up? Shoulder pads are even making a comeback, and this time they're meant to *really* empower women. Fashion changes. Meanings change.) As I'm typing, artificial intelligence (AI) is the hot topic, and is sure to reconfigure how society operates yet again. We like to call it "the other AI," since Applied Improvisation is the topic of this book. I wonder how the two AIs are coexisting as you read this book. One thing I know for sure—the need for the communication and connection you receive from Applied Improvisation is not going away.

For me, traveling the road of technology change highlighted a series of questions. How about communication skills? Are we still separating messy human from office worker? For so much of my early career, I was told to show up at the office without my whole human self—to leave my personal life at home. And I must say, this approach created a lot of turmoil for me and my colleagues. (I'm thinking of that great television thriller *Severance*, where people have been surgically divided so they only remember work while at work and only remember their personal lives when at home. Art expressing life? That separation doesn't function on the show, and our current, much less literal form of separation doesn't work in life.) We've made progress in some areas and not in others. As much progress as we can? I don't think so.

You might say that this focus on bringing only your work self to work creates a division, leading to personal confusion and a loss of identity. It's a "get 'er done" kind of toughness that creates disconnection. It skips through a lot of necessary human steps in an effort to focus solely on company goals. We need that heart-centered stuff. Space to be thoughtful, imaginative, and contemplative.

I'd worked in sales for years, and I had this great relationship with a colleague. (Sales and improv go together like peanut butter and jelly, by the way.) He called himself "Yang," and he called me "Yin." He acknowledged that he was impatient (that yang tendency), and he valued my patience and persistence in following up with prospects and customers. I also helped him manage his stress. He told me my support resulted in better health (physical and mental) for him, and also directly contributed to his having a terrific sales year. The two are linked.

As a sales coach, I've worked with hundreds of people just like "Yang." Some have been extremely challenging people with anxiety through the roof, and some are simply doing their best every day or leading with high spirits. A full mix. At times, people were in positions where they attempted to exert "power over" me. Many were colleagues or customers. I've noticed something in every single case: This need to dominate can frequently ease when you connect on a personal level in some way. You develop a bond. An authentic relationship. And that bond transfers delightfully into your day-to-day working life. Suddenly, there is joy in your day—you make room to understand one another, you give and receive ideas with ease. It's a kind of balance between relaxed, calm yin and quick, active yang—which is much needed in today's world—to achieve harmony. Balance.

Improv and "Yes, and" taught me how to communicate productively through the years. And now, I share those skills. There is one caveat, though: Because this world is filled with juxtaposition, sometimes you don't want to bring everything into the office. If you aren't comfortable sharing, if sharing means oversharing (you had a fight with your partner— potentially that can stay at home), or you want to keep your politics or religion to yourself, those may be examples of areas you may choose not to share. My point is—and my years of experience support this view—that when we find a relatable common ground with people and lead with empathy and understanding, oftentimes, work becomes more unified.

THE VALUE OF AUTHENTICITY AT WORK

According to a 2018 *Harvard Business Review* article (Aarons-Mele), statistics show that one in four adults struggle with mental wellness each year, and 18 percent of US adults have an anxiety disorder. Research also reveals that being authentic and open at work leads to better performance, engagement, employee retention, and overall well-being. Workplace cultures must provide space for the broad range of emotions we experience. Here's the bottom line, according to Harvard: $17 to 44 billion is lost to depression every year, while $4 is returned to the economy for every $1 spent caring for people with mental health issues.

The point is that bringing our whole selves to work—and working in an environment that celebrates that approach— results in a much stronger level of cooperation. That's because it all starts within us, and then leads us outward, toward how we show up and engage. We create a union of flow together—instead of receding into cut-off places that disconnect us from one another. We create that balance. Connection. Since improv helps us open up and bond in new ways, practicing improv creates an environment where we can lead with our authentic selves. Improv invites a heart-led approach to engaging at work. It invites vulnerable sharing and wholehearted offerings. It also offers a set of learnable skills that help each individual grow into a strong communicator. What if communication wasn't left to chance, luck, or fate? What if effective communication was an integral part of every person's education, training, and development?

The "Yes, and" Business Evolution

The "Yes, and" business evolution starts with your individual practice, expands to who you are as a leader, invites team participation, and supports your company and culture, leading to an open collaborative approach.

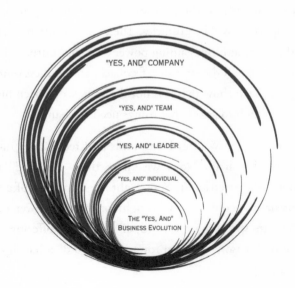

Why Improv?

Because one of the biggest challenges you have as a leader is your overall planning process, as well as how you implement your plans through a communications strategy. I'm talking about how you communicate with and involve people. And how you equip people on the learning and development pathway, as they collaborate together on actioning your goals. We all need to learn how to communicate more effectively. I'm talking deep, active listening, letting go of judgment and the need to be right, and learning to cooperate, give and receive, and build trust. You and your team will want to co-create together. And if you're a leader—and you are if you're reading this book—you want to fortify and empower your team.

These challenges are really opportunities. Chances to establish a new working order that starts with you. The process can be exciting and invigorating. Sometimes it's exhausting. That's okay. When we embark on the journey of conscious improvisational leadership, there will be obstacles. There's still a core message out there that competition, gaining power over, and burnout culture are the way. Yet all the statistics, feedback, and soulless outcomes of this approach show that it is not the way. We've been hustling for long enough to know that things need to change.

What can we do? We can bring tools and techniques into the workplace that help. Now, we know that "Yes, and" is not new, and I didn't create it. You might say I am part of a global movement of people who've caught on to the power of "Yes, and" and are spreading the word, all our voices offering a vivid collection of reasons why improv and "Yes, and" offer important skills training.

Applied Improvisation offers specific improvisational methods and techniques that have been established through widespread practice to help anyone become more innovative, more creative, and more successful in business—and in life. Improv can supercharge the development of strong communication skills. Building trust through spontaneous, powerful conversations and connections is a skill that can become part of your approach as a leader, and part of your team's as well.

You will learn how to:

- Stay in the moment, and stop thinking about what you are going to say next. Instead, fully listen, then respond in an impromptu, collaborative way.

- Be receptive to ideas that other people are offering, accept them with gratitude, and add your own ideas.

- Avoid interrupting and give space to any conversation so that everyone can be heard.

- Suspend judgment of other ideas so that you can remain open, particularly during brainstorming sessions.

- Say "Yes, and" to everyone's contribution to enhance creativity and the development of new ideas.

- Observe your verbal and nonverbal cues so you can develop confidence, and learn to participate fully.

- Replace words such as "but" and "should" with "and" to develop stronger communication and more positive relationships.

- Stop worrying and relax in high-stress situations.

- Show up for yourself and other people, offering your authentic voice to the conversation.

IMPROV HELPS TEAMS FLOURISH AND THE RESEARCH BEARS IT OUT

In recent years, more and more research has shown how improv helps teams communicate effectively and flourish. In her 2019 article for *Harvard Business Review*, "Using Improv to Unite Your Team," behavioral scientist Francesca Gino talks about how leaders can help their team feel heard, contributing to confidence and greater creativity.

Gino says, "In my academic research, I've looked at many different types of teams, at a wide variety of organizations all over the world. The group that communicated best, with everyone contributing and learning, wasn't in a corporate office park; it was in an improv comedy class." Why? Because improv offers simple techniques—rules of engagement—that can also benefit teams. Gino goes on to list a few in her article: "1. Instead of getting ready to talk, listen. 2. Don't assume you have all the answers. 3. Help everyone feel safe enough to contribute." The article shares how leaders who lead by encouraging curiosity—instead of judgment—are more impactful. People respond to a leader who is open to ideas from the team. This approach strengthens mutual respect and leads to innovation (Gino 2019).

Applied Improvisation, Applied

It's 2022, and my business partner Ralph and I are working with a client—a large national chain that makes and sells computer products. We're at the head office with fifty of their marketing and communications staff. A senior member of their leadership team saw Ralph and me deliver a keynote on improv at a leadership event a few months prior, and invited us to speak with their team on the merits of that presentation. This leader is worried about how the team is feeling as they return to the office after COVID. The team has a high level of anxiety around in-person interaction and needs help with team engagement. Their leader wants an event to help spark the transition.

On top of that challenge, the leader informs us that half of the team is more outgoing—creative, talkative communicators. The other half is more self-contained—technical, detail oriented, numbers focused. Most teams have a mix of all kinds of people. We need each other. And good teams have a blend. It's important. That's how all kinds of different projects get accomplished. We're told the team is having challenges around speaking up. Asking questions. Being positive disruptors.

At the start of the workshop, Ralph and I ask for a few volunteers to help out with some icebreakers (or ice-melters, which is a great term when you want to instill a sense of psychological safety within a group—inviting people to re-create relationships in a safer way). A couple of people saunter to the front. Ralph invites people to form into a line for a simple exercise: Word Association. One person says a word. Maybe "cat." The next person says whatever word pops into their head based on the word "cat." Perhaps "dog." And the line progresses in this way, with each person saying a word based on the last word they heard.

Every time we do this exercise (which is most workshops), some people get tentative with their word choice. Maybe they shrug their shoulders, as if to dismiss their choice. Or their voice goes upward, showing a lack of confidence. This is totally normal. Putting yourself out there is a little scary. Paying attention to your verbal and nonverbal cues takes practice. What made this day interesting too was that, as people got more comfortable with the exercises, they piped up with some vulnerable shares.

Suddenly, in the middle of the activity, one person says, "The first time I returned to work, I felt like my head was disconnected from my body—like a dream or weird state." That type of share can be a healing experience for someone. They've given voice to their fear. And even though sharing is a little frightening, this person speaks from the heart, and it is totally on the spot. Spontaneous. That's the power of improv: it creates an opening. From there, other people pipe up. The courage of one person leads to courageous moments for others. These are my favorite moments during more vulnerable improv trainings—when people set down their armor and share.

Later that day, we do an exercise called "Categories." This time, ten people come up to participate—and there is more enthusiasm. Yeah! I love it when, over the course of ninety minutes, people get cozy with improv. Everyone is laughing. Having fun. The Categories game is great because people get to have fun while they fail. This is an exercise that shows that failing is okay, and even important.

Everyone is in a line or semicircle, because their other team members are watching from the audience. Ralph gets a category from the audience, "types of flowers." Then he points at one person at a time, randomly—not in order. The person that Ralph is pointing at needs to say a type of flower, and it can't be a type of flower anyone has said so far. Nobody knows who Ralph will point at next. "Roses," "violets," "daisies," daffodils," "tulips." Pretty quickly, someone will run out of types of flowers to name, and that person will get buzzed out by the audience (their team members). "*Bzzzzz.*"

As they leave the exercise, they are encouraged to say disparaging comments about the exercise. "That exercise was terrible!" "Ralph is mean!" "Horrible time—you suck, Ralph!" People give voice to their feelings about failure—in a fun way. Ralph then continues with more categories like "names of countries," or "famous musicians." Whatever categories the audience shouts out.

When we debrief on this exercise, we talk about how failing is important. And the key is having each other's back. When we fail or make a mistake, and it's not the end of the world, we loosen up. We get out of fear and into creativity. We gain trust in one another. We're not afraid to speak up and be a part of the conversation. We learn that all ideas are good ideas, particularly when you're brainstorming. Exercises like Categories are a great start to opening up a team's dynamics so they begin to innovate in new ways. Stretch comfort zones. Get playful. Be spontaneous.

As we are leaving, a team member comes up to the car and says, "This workshop really helped me think about how I listen—really resonated with me. Thank you." You know the adage—if we can help one person, then that person is inspired to help another, and so on. That's how change happens across communities and around the world. Every time we improv train, it's rewarding. I've never left any event without someone coming up and saying something about how improv changed their outlook, even their lives.

Later, we also heard from this company's leaders who attended and participated in the event. The VP of Marketing said the office was still abuzz from the activities, which she acknowledged rarely happens with team events. Everyone had fun (laughing together creates synergy). Perhaps most importantly, this VP went on to say we really delivered. We were able to engage the whole team—in all their variety of roles and experiences—encourage participation, and build the learning that helped everyone return back to in-person engagement more smoothly. Evidence that this process works magic.

Training the Brain

To support the value of improv training, I also like to follow all the latest brain research. Improv trains the brain, and I like to consider the connections. I'm always looking at how brain health connects with improv—and it does. Dr. Judy Ho is a licensed clinical and forensic neuropsychologist whose 2022 book, *Stop Self-Sabotage*, caught my attention. Dr. Ho has a cool formula that I want to share with you because it ties into improv so well. She called it her LIFE acronym (Ho 2019), and it's all about how our brain self-sabotages as a way to stay safe. You know—how we can sometimes (or often) take our thoughts too seriously. And how we need to examine our thinking (through observation and awareness) to unlearn all those old stories we've been told through the years ("not good enough" is a big one). So, here's the LIFE acronym:

L: Low or shaky self-esteem
I: Internal beliefs from childhood
F: Fear of the unknown
E: Excessive need for control

As Dr. Ho was talking, I found myself saying "*Yes!*" And improv helps in all these areas. It's exercise for the brain that helps us dig into all this conditioning, allowing us to get in touch with—and overcome—fear. When you are encouraged to fail through improv—and given a safe space and a low-stakes place to fail—that's fun and full of play and laughter. That's when you stretch your comfort zone and help your brain get ready for the higher-stakes times. Improv helps you improve your self-esteem—it gets you present and in the moment so you can learn to observe your old thoughts and gain self-awareness. You learn to embrace fear, and particularly fear of failure. And as for control, improv is a team sport—it's all about give and take, and understanding we're all in it together.

As a leader, it's vital that you embrace your fear of failure. For yourself and your team. You've definitely seen your share of failure. How do you respond to failure? How do you talk with your team about the concept of failure? I'll bet that if you think about it, you'll see that most of your growth has been the result of mistakes. Same with your team. Once you see that failure is part of the pathway that will help you achieve your goals, you learn to let go of failure—even like it.

I remember when I was a teenager and gave my first short talk in front of a few hundred people. I was so nervous. I tried to make a joke—it fell flat. I was stumbling and my words weren't coming out right. I looked at my feet, sweating. As I left the stage in a puddle of embarrassment, everyone was looking at the floor. It was a mess. I felt demoralized and humiliated. Yet, I'm grateful for those shaky starts. As I persevered, even when I wasn't considered "good," I learned the power of carrying on. Today, I speak confidently, and I can regularly make a whole room erupt into laughter. More importantly, I focus, though not on myself. Rather, it's all about reaching my audience. Over the years, what happened is that I kept putting myself out there (through improv, Toastmasters, Speaker Slam, professional engagements, and performance). Did I fail? Yes, a lot. Do I still fail? Absolutely. What I've learned is that failing really doesn't matter—the point is to keep going. Keep on doing the thing.

Over time, you will find your unique voice, and remember: nobody can be you. You're the only you. So, the goal is to keep working on your authentic voice. Let "putting yourself out there" lead the way. Then, you come to realize that when you are speaking, writing, or presenting—being visible and vulnerable in any way—it's all about the impact felt by others. You learn to put your focus on the audience, and a sort of dance starts to happen, where you're listening to the energy and feedback in the room (verbal and nonverbal), and you're responding to whatever is happening in the moment. That's the power of improv, and that's how to overcome fear. Keep showing up and doing the thing. The more you do something, the more you will keep doing that thing in the future—and the better you will get at it. It's all a practice.

Feel the Fear

You may be familiar with Susan Jeffers's book *Feel the Fear and Do It Anyway*. I was rereading this communication classic because it has a strong focus on overcoming that fear state— one of improv's great benefits. Again, I found myself nodding and smiling when I read phrases like "Say *yes* to your universe" and "say *yes* to life" (Jeffers 2007). I found myself considering that a deeper explanation of yes is always required, because it's easy to believe you have to say yes to everything and bypass negativity or your own opinions. That's not the case. Saying yes means accepting. Accepting life and all its messy human stuff. Because once we accept something, that's when the breakthroughs come. It's resistance that creates conflict. Improv teaches us to let go of resistance and accept what is. Remember, that does not mean you have to agree. You simply accept and engage in conversation. Conversation with other people, and conversation with yourself too. "Yes, and" it.

Overcoming Ego

Jeffers describes our "box of thoughts," or our ego, as the "chatterbox," which makes us feel impatient. Chatterbox. Yep, that's right. It's a great practice to say to yourself, "I don't have to believe every thought I think." Or even soothe your mind: "Thank you for keeping me safe—we can think about that problem on Monday at 9:00 a.m., because right now I want to focus on this . . ." Leadership requires that we show up for our team as self-aware individuals who are observing ourselves, listening to other ideas, accepting offers, and staying open. Yes, we are making decisions—often quickly—every day. Yes, we are progressing toward shared goals and visions. Yes, there are always going to be conflicts, challenges, and disagreements. Yet, when we acknowledge one another—even when we don't agree—we can walk the path toward greater harmony. People want to be heard. Including you. When you listen, you hear—and you learn. Everyone grows. You overcome the rigid in favor of the flow. And that cooperation builds the all-important trust. As the leader, you set the tone.

How Improv Supports Your Leadership Goals

So, what is conscious leadership, anyway? How does it relate to being an improvisational leader? Conscious leaders practice self-awareness; they manage their company's growth by encouraging the people whose efforts propel the company forward. Rather than an ego-centric "me" mindset, they lead with an ensemble "we" approach. A conscious leader can be defined as one who takes responsibility for their actions and cultivates a desire to improve the lives of others alongside their own. They remain curious and open to exploring many viewpoints. Conscious leaders have integrity and practice bold candor when speaking. Yet, they remain respectful. Humble. Avoid gossip. Build trust. When it comes to failure, conscious leaders are adaptable. They know that circumstances change and that flexibility, a diversity of opinions, and unconventional solutions are necessary for growth.

Improv and "Yes, and" sensibilities support the conscious leader. Improv offers experiential training that helps teams stretch their comfort zones. It helps teams imagine. Ideate. When a conscious leader creates opportunities to brainstorm on a regular basis, without fear of judgment, and encourages many voices to share many ideas—that's when wonderful, wild changes become possible. Improv exercises create openings for people to learn in new ways, disrupting that judge in the brain that stops innovation. Improv creates team flow. Through the listening fundamentals and courage building of improv, reflection and understanding blossom.

In the coming chapters, we'll delve into more case studies, practices, exercises, and examples to help you bring the "Yes, and" foundation into your life—as an individual and as a leader. You'll learn to recognize "Yes, and" in people and to encourage in your team an openness to a new way of being. There will be challenges along the path. Life is meant to challenge you. That's how we grow. A transformation is underway, and you're part of it. Let's go! Yes, and . . .

Chapter Summary

- Improv helps people communicate more effectively.

- When you "Yes, and" one another, you stay open to ideas, inviting curiosity.

- Improv supports self-awareness and openness.

- Through improv, you can get out of your head and into the present moment.

- Embracing your fear of failure is vital on the pathway to growth and innovation.

- Improv helps you suspend judgment, develop your give-and-receive muscles, and build trust.

- Conscious leaders are also improvisational leaders who embrace improv to help teams imagine, collaborate, and open up.

CHAPTER THREE

Cultivating a "Yes, And" Team

The thing you fear most has no power. Your fear of it is what has the power. Facing the truth really will set you free.

—OPRAH

Ralph and I are facilitating at the Great Place to Work® Canada Annual Conference. It's 2019 and Great Place to Work® has been a valued partner for several years now. We support them by bringing improv skills to companies that are serious about being great workplaces. Companies that regularly seek input from their teams—including feedback through confidential employee engagement surveys—so they can identify actionable insights and improve company culture.

We tell the team of HR leaders, "The first rule is there are no wrong answers." Because in improv, there are no mistakes—only opportunities. And then we play a game called "What Are You Doing?," which is a crowd favorite. Partner A asks Partner B, "What are you doing?" Partner B makes something up on the spot: "I'm fishing!" That suggestion causes Partner A to start miming as though she were fishing. Uproarious laughter. While Partner B is fishing, Partner A then asks, "What are you doing?" and Partner B says a completely different activity: "I'm swimming." Now, Partner A starts miming swimming. More laughter.

The partners go back and forth—giving and receiving ideas—enjoying the playfulness of this verbal and physical scene. Sounds simple, right? Even silly. Appearances can be deceiving. These two colleagues are bonding. Experiencing one another in a new way. Developing their creativity muscles. They are saying "Yes, and" to each other's ideas unreservedly, letting go of the executive judge in the brain, opening up to fresh ideas. Expanding. Becoming flexible. Embracing collaboration. Learning that they've got each other's back. Building trust.

The Exercises Are the Teachers

You see, the exercises themselves do the teaching. They invite people to uncover new insights the experiential way. Let's face it: Nobody learns when you tell them what to do. Preaching and finger-pointing will take you nowhere. People have to feel growth in their bones—in their hearts, minds, and souls.

Yes, we match the exercises to business objectives. Yes, we design, facilitate, and guide the training, and then debrief after each exercise to show the value of the activity to the team. Yet, there is always some sparkling awakening—something that cannot be planned—that arises through the powerful improvisation of team spirit and dynamics. People are in the experience—doing it. Sense-making. That's where the transformation happens.

I'll take you to another scene: We're working with the whole team of a professional skin care company—sales, marketing, management, support staff, finance, everyone. This team is embarking on their annual plan and they're a little nervous. Many have never met before and have flown from various places around North America to be here. They want to embrace spontaneity, active listening, paraphrasing, and "owning a room" when it comes to sales and stakeholder relations. The team wants to develop their customer-facing skills, as well as their interactions with one another.

We engage with them for a couple of hours, opening them up to getting playful and saying "Yes, and" to one another. For this session, one of our exercises is "500-Year-Old Expert." It's totally hilarious. We break the team into smaller groups, and Ralph and I walk around the room facilitating, listening, and keeping the flow of the exercise going. Typically, we split the group into teams of four, and they choose a product to sell—let's say a flying machine. Each person "sells" the product for one minute. Person A talks about all the benefits and virtues of the product as though it were the 1500s—incorporating whatever language and ideas come to mind. Then, Person B talks about the product, again to the three partners who are listeners, as though it were the 1950s. The third person discusses the product as though it were present day, and the fourth pretends it's the future.

It goes something like this:

1500

"This most excellent flying machine before you. Considereth the virtues of said wheels and wings. Note the wonderful structure and sturdy steel parts. Let me demonstrate the fluid motion as I siteth in said cockpit and show movement of flying stick. Now, watcheth as I fly higheth in the skyeth and . . . won't you be my passenger and sit alongsideth me?"

1950

"This flying machine will get you back and forth to the office in record time. What was once a one-hour commute will now take fifteen minutes—twenty, tops. Allowing you to return home pronto in time for an excellent home-cooked six-course meal. Note the sleek aerodynamics—the most modern ever created. And, the special cockpit with full-screen, multi-push buttons."

Today

"You need to fly quickly between cities and around the world. This flying machine has the structure and aerodynamics to make your journey comfortable and speedy. Our state-of-the-art jet engines, spacious seating, and well-trained crew will make your experience unforgettable. Join us for a test flight and fly to your destination in class and style."

2080 and Beyond

This flying machine will help you time travel and move through multiple dimensions with ease. Note the laser energetic pulsating feature, which responds to your thoughts, letting you move from Shakespearean times of the past—where you can watch live Shakespeare plays in real time—on to the future, where you can simulate the state of the world based on programmable inputs."

Okay, sure, I made that up for this book—on the spot, I might add. That's what happens in improv. When people are in the moment, saying whatever comes up, there's a level of spontaneity and creativity that arises, getting people into a flow state and activating "on-the-spot" creation. Exercising this creative muscle opens people up, shifting mindsets and adjusting attitudes. It's an activation exercise that benefits people working in all kinds of positions, from sales to marketing to administration to management—everyone, really. The thing is, it gets you really present, inviting you to see things from another point of view. That's the grace of creation.

At times, teaching this exercise, we've had a room full of twenty groups of four, all exuberantly selling their fictional product to audiences from across time. Wonderful stuff. Again, you might ask, what's the point? So many professional skills are deepened in this deceptively goofy game. Opening. Opening to something new—another way. Imagining. Adjusting your conversations to the audience you have, rather than using jargon that makes you feel comfortable. Considering your audience's frame of reference, their language.

As Ralph and I were leaving, one of the planning managers ran up to us to say, "I just had to tell you how much we needed that. How much that helped us get into planning mode. How much that broke down barriers between us." Wonderful! The beauty of experiential work—opening, creativity, playfulness, "Yes, and!"

Your Dream Team

To determine how the transformative power of "Yes, and" can fit into your leadership plans, the first step is to dream. Let's begin by considering what your team needs. See if some of these aspirations resonate for you:

- *Purpose*—Your team has a strong sense of intention, supporting one another, understanding company mission and objectives, collaborating on an action plan, and working together on shared values.

- *Open Communication*—Your team feels empowered to tell one another how they are experiencing a project and their roles within it, and how they can be of use to one another—without feeling judged, manipulated, or scorned. Civilized disagreement—polite, friendly, and playful—is encouraged.

- *Consensus*—Your team actively works to hear differing ideas, arriving at decisions with unanimity while avoiding formal voting or easy compromises. Everyone plays a role in team decisions.

- *Stretching Comfort Zones*—Your team is encouraged—and motivated—to avoid the status quo and shake things up. Unapologetic disruptors have a place, consistently opening new avenues of creativity and innovation while breaking through silos.

- *Operating Skillfully in the Stakeholder Era*—Your team is equipped to communicate across functions, departments, branches, and companies—professionally representing your company, actively working with internal and external partners, vendors, and collaborators of all kinds. They are trusted, self-reliant, team players; courageous, upbeat, and strong.

- *Supporting Each Other as Human Beings*—Your team is able to achieve a high degree of success because they know they are fully supported by each other—and you, their leader. This is a team that helps one another out when the going gets tough. They do not participate in gossip or malicious and hurtful talk. Instead, they seek to rise up together—creating an environment of encouragement and loyalty, and a positive company culture.

Envisioning the qualities you want to see in your team offers you a kind of North Star, a way of staying oriented on your journey. You may want to mark this section or begin to draft your own Dream Team list as you let these concepts float in you. If you're a visual person, you may even find it fun to draw a picture of your team functioning in an ideal way. The more precise your goal, the easier it'll be for you to reach it.

> "As you navigate through the rest of your life, be open to collaboration. Other people and other people's ideas are often better than your own. Find a group of people who challenge and inspire you, spend a lot of time with them, and it will change your life."
>
> —Amy Poehler

Working with Wobbliness

Okay, you've got a vision of your Dream Team. Yet, like most leaders, you probably have a team that actually has a mix of good and not-so-helpful traits, ups and downs, consistent and inconsistent phases. How do you take a less-than-optimal reality and move it toward the idea you hold, the one that benefits all of you?

Here's a pattern I've seen in leaders and teams countless times over the past few decades. It goes something like this:

- Excited new leader builds team. Intentions are great and energy is high.

- Team is hired, they begin working, and spirits are up.

- Human beings start collaborating with varying degrees of success, depending on each individual's abilities, and particularly their ability to communicate.

- Some training programs are implemented, generally sporadically and with varying degrees of success.

- Results of the team are held up as either positive or negative examples of how they support revenue objectives (usually a mix).

- Regardless of the team's results, pressure is exerted from higher levels to perform better, stronger, faster—often with an emphasis on revenue results.

- Team members are loaded up with an overwhelming amount of tasks, leaving no space for effective communication, collaboration, or especially play.

- Trust erodes.

- Budgets are cut.

- There may be an attempt to get help from HR, and to implement a last-ditch effort at some kind of training program.

- Blame and finger-pointing begins.

- The team burns out, people stop working and communicating altogether, and performance plunges.

- The leader is fired, and the team is dismantled.

- Rinse and repeat.

I've worked with a lot of good people—great people. And some not-so-well-intentioned people too. Regardless of the individuals involved, this scenario plays out over and over again. Have you experienced some or all of the events I describe? I'd bet my vintage shoulder pad collection that despite your heartfelt best efforts, your team—and your company—aren't always functioning as you dreamed they would.

Sure, a good company culture needs a clear mission, values, diversity, authentic and present leaders, and ongoing professional development. Those things are givens.

Yet, a great company needs more.

A great company must:

- Create a culture of trust. (That means listening— listening is always your superpower.)

- Create a strong sense of company purpose (beyond profits).

- Support their employees' own personal purpose (beyond the scope of the company).

- Have the right people in the right positions.

- Allow people to fail—and even reward failure.

- Inspire—if you are not inspired by the leadership team, the company approach, and the company mission, then get out. Don't waste your time. Go somewhere where you will be inspired. Really. Life's too short.

I'm going to add one that I would like to see more often:

- A great company must, *must* give their employees *space*—space to learn, space to grow, space to be, and space to explore. Space is where the magic happens. A place where new ideas emerge. It's a creative place.

Without space, people wither, diminish, fall apart,
and burn out, and they ultimately stop working.
With *space*, people rejuvenate, and they are grateful.
Gratitude sparks loyalty. We humans all respond to
heartfelt caring. Give the gift of space and notice how
vitality emerges.

Improv supports the point that "giving space" is important to human well-being. It's because you are in the moment when you improvise—fully present. Since improv trains people to collaborate through play and get comfortable with making mistakes, an environment of "speaking up" is also encouraged. That's why holding one improv session and then going back to business as usual doesn't fully create a shift. Although most people will fondly remember that improv experience as a "one-off," it isn't a commitment to change behavior.

Whether you're overseeing a company or a team within one, if you want to move in the direction of realizing your Dream Team, it's vital that you build in the elements that keep team members feeling enlivened, valued, and free. Take another look at that list of qualities in a truly great company. Are there changes you can make to nourish the spirits of your team? And is there a way to increase your team's experience of *space*?

So how do you get from burnout to breakthrough? I would like to present you with a new frame of reference. Something to dream on. Can you envision a team environment that's playful, inspired, and creative, *and* focused, high-performing, and results-oriented? There's a kind of high energy to that vision, wouldn't you say? When you focus on your team's well-being, plus their learning and development, and combine that with communication around your purpose and goals, you ignite passion. It's the improvisation way. You want to enlist the type of training that involves leaders and teams in creating your company's vision while conveying a sense of purpose. A place where work and soul meet. To create this deeper level of connection you want to design an environment of trust. You want to help people practice:

Active Listening—The practice of improv works this muscle to help you really listen to what another person is saying, rather than planning your response while they're talking. When you truly listen, people feel seen and heard, and you uplevel the energy and mood of your conversation.

Collaboration—When you experience improv, you learn to "give and receive" during conversations and stay open to diverse perspectives. Your communication becomes a co-creation through which you truly listen and enter the flow of sending and accepting ideas.

Confidence & Courage Building—Improv teaches that it's a benefit to embrace being human over appearing perfect. People tend to connect with other people who "let go of their armor" and show up in a safe and supportive way. Letting go of perfectionism and opening yourself to being vulnerable, in certain situations, goes a long way.

Communication—Improved communication skills may be viewed as an overarching benefit of improv. For example, communication is enhanced through active listening and increased awareness in the moment. When you are present, spontaneous, and responsive—letting go of fear of failure—you rely on what's happening in the "now," beyond any judgment or assumptions. This focus on "thinking on your feet" skills trains and reinforces effective communication.

Creativity—Since improv supports risk-taking and coming up with ideas in the moment, creativity naturally emerges from this open-flow state. By expanding your comfort zone and inviting in failure, you are sure to find that new ideas spring forth. Improv gets the mind into that lovely present state that trains the brain for the adaptable skill of creativity.

Empathy—Through active listening and being in the moment, improv supports empathy, helping you understand and share the feelings and experiences of another person. You see a situation from another point of view and can respond by tuning in to situations more effectively.

Judgment—Improv helps you suspend judgment, so you can stay open to new ideas. Rather than getting defensive or taking on a negative attitude, you soften your approach and heighten your awareness. Through improv, you hone your acceptance skills and avoid responding in a "knee-jerk" way.

Nonverbal Communication—Through improv, you gain self-awareness around how you stand (relaxed, arms at your side and not folded), your eye contact (maintain without staring), and overall posture. By observing your nonverbal communication, you also gain confidence, as your body language supports your tone and manner.

Perspective Taking—Slightly different from empathy, perspective taking means you can put yourself in the place of another person, while recognizing their context, experience, and beliefs. You may not take on the "feelings" of another; however, you can understand where they're coming from.

Playfulness—Play is at the heart of improv, as a way to connect and build trust. You pay attention to the present moment with curiosity and kindness. Improv is a playful practice that offers a "low-stakes" way to prepare for "high-stakes" events.

Presence—Improv helps you cultivate presence, so you show up as your authentic self in the moment. When you are present, can hold space for another, and deeply attune with a person's experience, that person feels heard. You have an opportunity to bridge differences and find common ground.

Storytelling—Improv helps you prepare for unscripted conversations by developing your storytelling skills. As you construct a story in real time, without advance notice of your topic or a script, you gain courage and express yourself more fully in the moment.

"Thinking On Your Feet" Skills—When you engage in improv, you "train the brain" to adapt and get flexible when faced with all kinds of situations. Improv supports the agile approach to communication—you develop the impromptu skills needed to embrace the unknown.

"Yes, And": The Foundational Principle of Improv— "Yes, and" is a pillar of improv, and it is an acceptance principle. When you learn the technique of "Yes, and," you learn to listen, accept what another is saying, and build on their idea with your own idea. "Yes, and" does not mean you have to agree; it means you are hearing and accepting—offering respect for other ideas.

So, What's a Conscious Leader to Do?

Maybe those difficult scenarios don't apply to you so much. Let's say you're a leader, and you work at a pretty good place, maybe even in a really great environment. You're developing the structures and learning and development programs that every company needs to excel. You're creating a culture of respect and integrity and encouraging personal and professional growth. Strong values. You're doing all the things.

When it comes to training, you've created a dynamic series of programs with a focus on flourishing—keeping employees engaged, motivated, and supported. Inspiring curiosity. Opening minds. Idea generation is flowing.

When you think about it, working at a company can feel a little chilly when the focus is only on keeping up with the market, cash flow, and revenue. While that's certainly important, because without profits there is no company, it's really the people that make a good company great. And not only people—the right people in the right jobs doing the right things. It comes down to teams, and teams are made up of individuals. Sounds simple, and yet the human focus can get lost in the shuffle of revenue growth targets.

People grow, find new jobs, move along—that's a natural evolution. It's a good thing. As your team is changing, growing, and replenishing, you want to be providing a healthy environment—bring in that balancing yin, while keeping some of that yang too. Your team is an ecosystem, and it needs a lot of interacting ingredients—like give and receive, active listening, courage building, and getting away from judgment, fear, and the need to be right. Your team needs "Yes, and," not only because it buoys their professional well-being, yet also because "Yes, and" combats the chill. Improv in the workplace celebrates the humanness of those hard at work in your teams. And as a conscious leader, honoring the humanity of people on your teams is central to your role.

Chapter Summary

- When it comes to improv, the exercises are the teachers.

- Your Dream Team needs you—as a leader—to support an open, "Yes, and" environment.

- Create your own Dream Team checklist and notice how improv can support your team's growth.

- Build trust and create a sense of purpose to inspire your team.

- You and your team need to understand that failure can be tolerated (and even encouraged in certain situations) if you want to overcome fear and help your team thrive.

- Giving people space results in vitality and greater creativity. Improv helps open a pathway to space through the practice of presence.

- Through improv training, people adopt a set of valuable communication skills that support employee engagement while positively impacting company culture.

CHAPTER FOUR

The World's New "Yes, And" Leaders

We see the world, not as it is, but as we are—or,
as we are conditioned to see it. When we open
our mouths to describe what we see, we in effect
describe ourselves, our perceptions, our paradigms.

—Stephen Covey

When "No" Is Toxic

In serving a vast array of clients, from technology to packaged goods, finance, education, nonprofits, government agencies and departments, and just about everything in between, I have seen a lot of different leadership styles. A couple of years ago, while working with a start-up technology company for a few months, I witnessed the owner say "No!" to his team at least ten times whenever I was in the room. I counted. He said "No!" hundreds of times during the period I was there. It was one long, nonstop "No." And his "No" was menacing, angry, frustrated, and mean. Belittling, actually. What we call low-vibe communication. He was constantly telling everyone that they were wrong about everything. The team was scared, disoriented, and totally shut down. This team was a dysfunctional group of employees living in fear of their leader. Participation was low and nobody was contributing ideas, because all they would hear would be "No!"

This company's focus was heavy on technology and light on human connection.

And they all accepted his behavior as the norm. They were never surprised and displayed no emotional responses, and when speaking to me privately, they said, "That's just the way it is." I was flabbergasted, though not shocked; I'd seen this sort of leader plenty of times, and this company owner clearly had little to no training on how to collaborate with people. He was a technology wunderkind who had created a product. He didn't know how to play well with others. He certainly wasn't listening. He thought he had all the answers and was right all the time, and led from this place—this inability to accept critical feedback. On top of that, he lacked respect and empathy for his team.

I was observing the situation and, frankly, taking notes. This guy was a great example of toxic leadership. I wish I could say he was the only one. He's not. If you've spent time in the workplace, you've experienced a toxic leader. You know the type. Earlier in this book, we discussed how the word "No" has incredible benefits in the right situations. However, in situations like this one, when the company should be creating a dynamic, effective team built on trust, "No" is weaponized, and it wreaks havoc.

The toxic boss brought his baggage into the office. You know, a lack of self-awareness and a lot of power-hungry, "blame the victim" behavior. To anyone who's been bullied or belittled by a toxic boss, you know how this cycle of abuse undermines your confidence, makes you fearful, and eventually impacts your effort in negative ways. Ultimately, companies lose when they overlook the behavior of a toxic boss. Their best employees leave. Turnover goes way up. Because people often quit their bosses, not their jobs. Those who stay are in for an environment where destroyed morale and sinking employee engagement are sure to be the norm. And for companies who do stay the course, look out for a reduced profit margin. Unhappy teams do not produce great results.

GALLUP 2023: THE MAJORITY OF THE WORLD'S EMPLOYEES ARE "QUIET QUITTING"

Around the world:

- 23% of employees are thriving at work. (Engaged.)

- 59% are quiet quitting. (Not Engaged.)

- 18% are loud quitting. (Actively Disengaged.)

Gallup has found one clear answer: Change the way your people are managed. In their 2023 "State of the Global Workplace Report," Gallup estimates that "low engagement costs the global economy $8.8 trillion." The report goes on to say that it's up to leaders to impact employee engagement, and cites team building, regular check-ins and conversations, and a supportive environment as key. Constant communication. And that means listening. When people experience camaraderie, purpose, and connection at work, they prosper. Leaders want to have an active role in this type of engagement, as it's not only an HR mandate. It's a leadership directive too, the report confirms.

Wherever you are in the world, whatever year, check out this Gallup poll and read up on your region at gallup.com/workplace.

There is endless research to underscore that companies must make employee care part of their culture for the long term. What is "employee care"? Programs and training that help people thrive. That let people bring their whole selves into work and feel supported—because suffering and struggling employees, as Gallup and other reports show, are more likely to be diagnosed with depression, anxiety, and disease—and have higher rates of absenteeism. Bottom line: lower productivity.

Yes, the Gallup report will continue to be released each year with new evidence and suggestions. Personally, I welcome the day when those statistics improve, when more people report they are flourishing, and well-being is celebrated. This shift will mean that conscious leaders are also on the rise. People are championed to grow. Company culture recognizes that the well-being of each individual also supports their mission, values, and, yes, revenue. The widespread understanding of how you can draw a direct line from toxic leadership and poor company culture to a decline in employee retention and revenue could by itself transform the working world. Not only is attention to employee welfare the right thing to do, it also makes smart business sense.

Working on Purpose

We now know—through years of research, from Gallup and so many others—that good (and great) leadership requires deep listening, giving and receiving of ideas, and leading with a kind of self-awareness that encourages people to prosper while also inspiring people through the leader's vision. People excel profoundly and do their greatest work when leaders encourage a sense of purpose, a sense that they are contributing to something that is bigger than themselves. By practicing innovative training strategies such as improv techniques together, we learn to care more about how we experience our profession, build faith with our colleagues, and find joy in our place in the world. We are inspired by strong, empathetic leadership.

The "No" guy at this technology company wasn't even what I would call a "bad" guy. He had many fine qualities. He needed help. He needed a coach, training, direction, and a new way to interact. He needed someone to mentor and guide him. Here he was, the big-time owner of a start-up technology software company, and he was leading with fear. His big worry was profits and how fast could he get them. That is the world he knew. And that is the world we have created, in many places. He was flailing—and he didn't even know it. Where was the self-reflection and emotional intelligence? Undeveloped. Where were his training and development programs? Nonexistent. He was an unconscious leader, leading from that ego-centric "me" place.

I wish I could say I turned this team around—I could not. This guy was entirely inflexible. He definitely wasn't about to listen to me either. And, as the owner of a start-up, he could go his own way and continue spreading his "I'm the owner, I'm right all the time, and everyone else is wrong" poison. Am I being too harsh? I don't think so. Unfortunately, this dynamic plays out time and time again across the world in all kinds of situations— personally and professionally—at small companies and large ones, in every industry, all the time. And it comes down to poor leadership—leaders and bosses who have not acquired the skills of self-awareness. This approach is what they've been taught, and it's what they are mirroring and modeling too.

As a leader, you've got to have the courage to look yourself in the eye and say, "I have blind spots. I need continuous coaching and training. And my team deserves ongoing support and skills training too." It's not a nice-to-do; it's a have-to-do.

The Makings of a Great Leader

How are we going to turn this around? Perhaps one conscious leader at a time. You're here. Let's walk along the pathway together.

The thing is, a great leader doesn't become a great leader overnight. We've talked about how developing self-awareness is a lifelong practice. Whether you consider yourself a conscious leader now or you're still on the path, there are always ups and downs. Life is a roller-coaster ride with all kinds of detours, rises and falls, flips and spins. For the developing conscious leader, challenges and failures are part of the pathway to transformation. And while life is busy shaking you up and throwing you into free fall, you want a personal development plan in place to help you prosper. Part of your plan has got to be a commitment to lead with heart. Another part must be to embrace an improvisational approach to leadership.

> "Improvisation is probably one of the two or three cardinal skills for businesses to learn . . ."
> —John Kao

A Conscious Leader Is Also an Improvisational Leader

We understand that the old way of leading, the unconscious approach, is driven by the ego and outdated conditioning, such as learned behaviors passed on from other poor leaders, or learned behaviors in general. We met those leaders both at the start of this book and in this chapter—*my way or the highway*. Those aren't the only leadership challenges, of course. Some leaders micromanage, play favorites with certain staff, are overly critical, or lack confidence and are indecisive themselves. Maybe there's a lack of transparency, lack of direction, lack of listening skills. Hey, nobody's perfect. Improv teaches that perfection isn't even the goal. Instead, the goal is self-awareness: having your own coaching program to help you develop better habits and approaches, such as a mindfulness program. Such as improv. When you're working on yourself, you create space to become that stronger leader. A conscious leader leads with an inclusive "we" approach. This person knows that nothing works without a strong, cohesive team. You want to build a dynamic, purpose-motivated ensemble. And you want to lead with integrity, letting your team take the spotlight. Sometimes, becoming a strong leader requires unlearning misguided ways of being.

Overcoming Ego

For developing leaders, the number one shift that changes everything is the movement away from "me" to "we." Getting out of your assumptions and judgments, getting away from the need to be right. When a leader takes credit for the ideas of others or dismisses a team's achievements without acknowledging them, the team feels reduced and demoralized. The "Yes, and" way is all about making the team look great. When you focus on creating an ensemble where everyone looks good, everyone wins. Morale shoots up. People feel supported and motivated. Overcoming ego and placing your attention on the well-being and success of people will take you far.

Self-Awareness

The conscious leader is self-aware. This practice of self-observation—continuously observing how you show up—leads to real change. It's a kind of "bringing it all together." You—a conscious leader on the rise—observe your actions, how you speak, your verbal and nonverbal cues. You are mindful of how your ego is manifesting. (Are you leading with "me" or "we"?) You pay attention to your physical, emotional, mental, and spiritual facets. Your heart is in the game—empathy and perspective taking are part of your communication style. And you communicate continuously. These approaches lead to the agility described above. You adapt more easily to change because you've cultivated a climate in which everyone is interconnected—improvising and "Yes, and–ing." And you naturally overcome fear because you're sharing successes, taking responsibility for and learning from failures, and letting everyone know you've got their backs. That's trust.

Showcasing Your Team's Strengths

Understanding how each individual contributes to your team and what each person's strengths are helps you employ their specialized skills appropriately. People are more confident when they feel they are contributing their full knowledge and capabilities on a team.

A troublesome approach I've noticed through the years is when company leaders repeatedly reassign people to new tasks outside their area of knowledge. Instead of looking closely at a person's capabilities, these leaders appoint people to jobs based on gaps in the company. This displacement of personnel typically results in discomfort and an inability to do the job. When leaders look at the gaps in a company and ignore the actual skills of each employee, moving people around becomes ineffective. Instead, an improvisational leader leverages the talents of each person and works with them on an individual learning and development plan. They listen to their team members and pay attention to where they want to be, where they will flourish. They help their team members build new skills that complement their talents.

Another rigid approach to leading is expecting everyone on the team to have the same set of skills. People are coming to a company with vastly divergent backgrounds, abilities, and brains. The improvisational leader allows people to lead with their strengths and creates an environment of support. Each person helps another, and they fill in each other's gaps. The sales development team at one of my longtime prior clients, an international software company, has an open chat dialogue online all day. Yes, they catch up on the weather, share some memes, and have a laugh. That's important bonding. They also let everyone know how they're doing on the job ("Got another sales appointment!" or "Working on my customer list today.").

If someone needs technical help—or any kind of assistance—they post about their need in the chat. Someone always jumps in to lend a hand. By the way, the leaders of the team are also active in this daylong conversation, posting fun, inspirational sayings ("Teamwork is the dreamwork" or "When one succeeds, we all succeed."). This constant chitchat is super important, as it creates team harmony and an environment of respect and trust. It also helps everyone lead with heart.

Leading with Heart

Leading with heart means leading with awareness. It's a "Yes, and" approach. Back to "I'm listening to you, you're listening to me, even if we don't agree." Leaders who lead with heart have empathy. They can put themselves in another's shoes. And, if the empathetic approach of understanding another's feelings isn't the preferred approach in a certain situation, one can apply perspective taking. Through perspective taking, you come to understand how a situation appears for someone else, even if your own view is different (check the glossary for more on empathy and perspective taking). This ability to be vulnerable is a critical leadership trait. It breaks through the hierarchy and the titles, showing the leader's human side. It's courageous to be vulnerable, and courage is integral to the conscious improvisational leader. When you show up as vulnerable, you create connection, and people will follow your lead.

Communication

Regular communication with your team is vital to your success and the success of your team. Do you hold weekly or biweekly meetings with each team member? Monthly meetings with the whole team? Those may be standard. Something beyond that standard, which gives everyone a chance to speak up (and gets people into the practice of speaking up), is regular team brainstorming sessions. During these get-togethers, people can say what's on their mind, bring new ideas forward, and get a chance to share. These sessions may be formal or informal (or a blend of both). Structured or unstructured. Whatever your team needs. Beyond generating new ideas and solutions to problems, these discussions offer a chance for everyone to connect. It's easy to get caught up in the day-to-day effort and get a kind of tunnel vision around what you're doing. Instead, a constant understanding around how you fit into the bigger picture can also lead to breakthroughs around how things are being done.

Often, a gap exists between leader and team because the leader is off in one direction, fulfilling mandates from above, while the team is working away on programs and tasks. Sometimes, the leader has a whole new direction they're supposed to be moving in, and the team doesn't even know. It can take months (years in larger companies) to connect these differing mandates. It's important to be constantly communicating, reviewing and revising approaches, and making sure everyone's working toward the same purpose and goals. Regular communication between leaders and team members likewise provides a needed feeling of connection. This improvisational focus on communication creates an agile environment.

> "Great leaders communicate and great communicators lead."
>
> —Simon Sinek

Agility

Perhaps your company has decided that becoming agile is a directive. The idea is to be nimble and responsive to change, to adapt quickly. As a leader, you want to lead with agility. How? The constant flow of feedback between you and other leaders—and your teams—creates movement. You stay open to viewing situations and challenges from a variety of angles. You encourage team members to contribute ideas (back to regular brainstorming sessions), and you understand that a constant sharing results in creativity that supports the company as a whole. The agile company empowers teams and endorses accountability, transparency, and collaboration. As a great teacher of how to be nimble, improv is a wonderful complement that supports agility.

Overcoming Fear

A big part of how you show up as a leader is how you encourage people. What happens when people make mistakes? Do you say, "You really blew it," or do you ask, "What did you learn?" These two responses are miles apart. The "What did you learn?" style is the approach of a conscious leader, and it comes from that "we" mentality that we're all in this together. We have each other's back. When mistakes happen, we're going to work through them. Yes, obviously at times you need to manage a difficult employee scenario, such as if someone isn't functioning or able to do their job. That's an HR issue, and that person needs support. Here, I'm talking about a leader sharing successes with the team and encouraging everyone to check their fear of failure.

Helping your team tackle this fundamental human challenge can be as simple as fostering an environment where speaking up in meetings, sharing ideas, and engaging in a positive "give and receive" are celebrated. An improvisational conscious leader honors the messiness of effort, even when errors occur, since processing missteps is central to the process of evolving as individuals and as a group.

Improv is so wonderful for exploring the idea that failure is often good—the pathway to growth and creativity. I was reading journalist and author Elizabeth Gilbert's book *Big Magic: Creative Living Beyond Fear* and I was struck by her "Fear is Boring" chapter. She talks about how her fear "never changed, never delighted" and "was the same thing every day" (Gilbert 2015). We don't want to eat kale every day, do we? (Hmm . . . maybe—they do say kale is good for you). You get my drift. Hey, sometimes fear keeps us safe, and we've been talking about that important point here in this book. When it comes to stretching our comfort zones, though, taking a peek at our fear can lead to beautiful new horizons in life and work.

How Improv Supports the New Leader

Incorporating improv into your leadership style means you are disrupting repetitive patterns of behavior and inspiring people to try something new. Improv's experiential activities help change attitudes. When people get comfortable imagining beyond their current situation, new ideas pop up. And when they participate in exercises that let them play with their status—high or low— they also get to play with how confident they feel. This focus on playfulness, on learning new things, breaks through hierarchy and biases. Most importantly, it humanizes everyone.

There's nothing like the effect of "Yes, and" to help a conscious leader actualize their dreams for their teams. While everyone participating is busy having fun, as you have seen in these pages, serious growth is taking place. The team wins, and the new conscious improvisational leader wins too.

And What About the Big Picture?

The toxic "No" start-up boss I discussed at the beginning of this chapter could have helped himself and his team by bringing in developmental training, including improv training. Sadly, he stayed stuck. How do you tell a leader they need to change? I believe that's the job of other leaders. Gentle nudges toward external training can help. How about a story of the time you changed your own behavior by adopting new practices? Storytelling invites reflection and change. As you grow, you set an example for those around you. If we all add some self-awareness techniques into our lives, we help uplevel communication skills person by person, team by team, community by community. Over time, communities extend to different cities, different countries—to the world. You plant a seed of awareness, and while you impact others, you continue to blossom too.

Welcome to the Path

Now, you're on the improvisational leadership path, and you're getting clear on how to take action. You're connecting your head to your heart, and you're prepared to examine your inner self on a regular basis. That means a regular check-in on how your ego and conditioning are showing up, and whether you are consistently operating under a "we" strategy that benefits your team. You are leading with heart, which takes courage. You transcend the easy way of saying "No" to people, of moving forward with only your own goals in mind. Instead, you hold a compassionate view and empathy for the teams you lead. You're sharing stories and encouraging team members to do the same. That's part of the magic of improv. Improv opens us up, invites us to be present in the moment, and encourages vulnerable shares.

Perhaps most importantly, you're listening. Flexing that "Yes, and" style that makes you an improvisational leader too. You've invited improv techniques into your training programs, and people are beginning to thrive. Maybe people in the office are starting to say "Let's 'Yes, and' that," when they have a challenge to move through or an idea to discuss. You're inviting people with all kinds of differing abilities, personalities, and life experiences to collaborate. Your purposeful team is becoming stronger by the day. Everyone is contributing with creativity and a newfound confidence. You have become a "Yes, and" leader, and that all started when you embraced becoming a "Yes, and" individual. That's what the next chapter is about. Let's go!

Chapter Summary

- While the word "No" is important in certain situations, it can be a toxic choice when creating a dynamic, connected team built on trust.

- Every leader needs continuous coaching and training because we all have our blind spots.

- Every team deserves ongoing support and skills training—it's not a nice-to-do; it's a have-to-do.

- To create an agile team, you want to lead with heart, overcome ego and conditioning, and invite in courage.

- Supporting your team with effective communication, empathy, and perspective taking is a winning combination.

- Overcoming fear of failure is important to your team's success and leads to greater creativity.

- Self-awareness is the name of the game, and you want to make it a practice.

CHAPTER FIVE

The "Yes, And" Individual

Get the inside right, and the outside will fall into place.

—ECKHART TOLLE

How can improv help you as an individual, so that you communicate better as a leader, a team member, and an all-around self-aware person? As you are out and about in the world, you're always wearing a lot of hats—constantly shifting your identity as you converse with this person, connect with that group, or simply stand in line at the grocery store. Everything you do invites you to bring a certain aspect of yourself to each encounter. And improv techniques, along with the power of "Yes, and," can be practiced on your own too, to support personal growth. I like to call it a moment-by-moment practice where you get into the habit of observing yourself— and your reactions—in any set of circumstances. Because how you show up in one part of your life impacts how you show up in everything. This focus on individual growth led me to think about my own personal development.

Life can be a roller coaster at times. Who hasn't had a terrible crisis, a spectacular downward spiral, or a profound inner struggle? I know I have. How about you? Nobody escapes life's adversities. I have to say that leaning on books to guide me, joining groups, and different kinds of training have really helped. Part of this training was actually my hobby: improv. So,

I've been able to develop my personal communication skills all along. Of course, I also had all kinds of extensive training within companies, and the learning never ends.

I can recall many times when life seemed overwhelming, I felt stuck in a rut, or I was in the midst of a crisis. Challenging experiences are part of life, after all. Yet, improv was there to guide me with its mindfulness principles. I've been able to bring improv techniques and the practice of "Yes, and" into my personal and working worlds for decades. I've found that how you appear as an individual in your life has a direct impact on how you appear as a leader for your team.

I still remember everything about the first time I actively participated in improv. It was February 1987, and I know this because I still have the ticket. As I mentioned earlier, it was a drop-in class at Harbourfront on Toronto's lakefront and the improv show was called Theatresports. I was hooked.

The main reason for my hooked-ness was this dazzling and immediate sense of community. When I walked into that class and started "clap focusing" with all these supportive, creative people, I felt connection. Little did I know that one of the main reasons I felt so connected is because the improv exercises themselves make you feel that way. When you stand in a circle with a group of people and everyone starts clapping toward you, giving you eye contact, laughing, and getting playful—it's contagious. It's "Yes, and" for the soul.

My initial foray into improv was all about the performance side of things, yet as we've been discussing, the principles of performance and nonperformance improv are the same—the outcomes simply have different applications. I was watching

The Kids in the Hall, Saturday Night Live, and *SCTV*—and then came Theatresports, and the improv class where I learned to try out what I'd been seeing.

I didn't really understand the mechanisms behind the exercises and my feelings in response to collaborative learning—not yet. I was in the "experiencing" stage, and that's a beautiful place to be. Just experiencing without overthinking. Without getting bogged down in too much information, I was able to get into the experiential flow. That's where the learning is. On a personal level, getting improv into my bones made me feel free. Perhaps it's because you can't be anywhere else except in the moment when doing improv—presence is guaranteed.

Along the way, I was beginning to recognize how improv could be good for the workplace too—those epiphanies naturally evolved as I progressed. You could say that this process kind of just happened to me. Although I didn't know it, I wasn't alone—not at all. Improv for corporate and team building was on the rise. It's been waiting for its moment all along. I'm here to say that its time has fully arrived.

As I write this, I'm wondering if you've ever taken an improv class. If so, I'm sure your own memories about how improv affected you are coming to mind. If not, this chapter is about how you can begin this journey. Either way, the "Yes, and" movement that's been growing for decades starts with you. How you practice "Yes, and" and involve this training in your life will impact people. And as you—a leader—bring improv skills to yourself and your team, the results will grow and deepen. Let's "Yes, and" this . . .

The Individual "Yes, And" Practice

Whether you've tried improv or not, it's fair to say it's an ever-evolving practice. Every improviser I know—whether a performer, teacher, corporate facilitator, or all of the above—has struggled to make "Yes, and" a regular part of their lives. Sometimes, it's easy to "Yes, and" on stage and then drop "Yes, and" when we get back into the messy, complicated, human parts of our lives.

Since I've been in both the improv community and the corporate arena, it's been fun to watch my different worlds collide as improv training exercises uplevel the working world. Why is this happening? Because we all need the practice of "Yes, and." Whether at home, at work, on stage, driving in your car, or at the grocery store, we need to continuously focus on those communication skills. On how we communicate with ourselves, as well as other people.

Think about how you get up in the morning, start your day, and show up for your team. Are you always in a rush? Do you get in your car and yell at other drivers on your way to the office? How do you treat service workers at the coffee shop or grocery store? How do you speak to your partner, children, and neighbors? How do you speak to yourself?

All of these scenarios run into each other throughout your day. That's why the listening and observing techniques of improv, combined with the communication flow of "Yes, and," can be such useful approaches to inform you. Of course, even though you're practicing all the time, you'll also find developing your self-awareness restful. Because when you level up your own communication skills, everything around you improves too. As you consistently practice being in the moment, rush turns into calm, and rather than identifying with the future and past too much, you return to center—to the now.

Competition, Comparison, Impostor Syndrome, and Perfectionism

We all struggle with emotional states that trouble us, and the feelings that accompany comparison with other people are both painful and universal. We've got lots of approaches to addressing them too, from mindfulness meditations to a walk in the park with our beloved dog. Or if you're a cat person (like me), cuddling up to your kitty friend. It's worth exploring how the gifts of improv can offer a different slant on the turmoil within us.

I was in a meeting with—let's call her Mary—and we were talking about how Yes Unlimited could bring improv skills to her team of two hundred. Out of the blue, she blurted, "I have impostor syndrome." This happens a lot. People are sometimes more willing to reveal their feelings of inadequacy to a complete stranger. The stakes are lower. I actually felt honored when Mary shared. I quickly wondered what I could say in the next two minutes that might open a possibility for Mary—plant a seed of confidence.

Here's one approach: The thing about impostor syndrome is that it's rooted in old conditioning—ego. It's a feeling of "not good enough" that has plagued humankind for eons. How do we overcome the feelings of self-doubt we all have at times? The answer is complex, and it's likely that many answers are rooted in our pasts. In part, the solution is about unlearning and rewiring the brain. When I hear people comparing themselves to other people, or are in negative competition mode, I know they are really feeling "less than" about themselves. These emotions are often combined with perfectionism, or a sense that we have to do everything right all the time. We've all exhibited these tendencies at times. In making a change, a key step is to start with observation. Pay attention to yourself and notice how you feel when you feel like an impostor. Let the emotion be. Remember, feelings come and go. Observing and accepting lets the feeling dissipate, giving you courage and strength. Over time, you can stand tall, rooted in your own individual strengths, realizing that your unique voice—with all its imperfections—is truly beautiful.

Here are a few techniques derived from improv—and mindfulness practices—that can help with the feelings Mary revealed, as well as many other states of distress:

- *Focus on Other People, Rather than Yourself*—Get out of your head and show up in the moment. This practice is also a top presentation skill. When we put our attention on our audience, we put the spotlight on what they want to hear from us.

- *Believe with All Your Heart*—Embrace affirmations that help your brain focus on the positive, getting you out of fight-or-flight mode.

- *Get Playful*—Invite your unique gifts into the world. What wants to be born through you? Make space in your life through a vision board, doodling in your journal, singing. Try an improv class. (Had to get that one in here.)

- *Develop an Alter Ego*—Some people call this a "fake it until you make it" attitude. For some people, being brave starts with adopting a new persona. Pretend you are courageous, and before you know it, you will be.

- *Focus on Your Breathing*—When you observe your breathing, you can't really overthink. Put all your attention on your inhales and exhales, and slow down so your parasympathetic nervous system tells your brain that you're safe.

- *Foster New Habits*—What is something you really want to achieve? Bring it into your day. Start with five minutes, and see how this short amount of time grows. You can also get into habit stacking. For example, right after you brush your teeth or have your coffee (or whatever part of the day is right for you), add in your new habit. Then your brain will associate this new habit with your activity, and it will begin to stick.

- *Show Up*—Keep the promises that you make for yourself. Get up. Do the thing. And, when you don't—be gentle with yourself. Start over. I always say "The more you do something, the more you will do that thing." The more you show up for yourself, the more you *will* show up for yourself.

- *Practice Being Grateful*—Spread your arms wide, like the sales group I led and shared about in chapter 2. Say "I'm grateful" out loud. Write down three things you are grateful for every day. When you think a negative thought, write down six things that you also feel positive about, to offset the brain's focus on fear (our natural defense mechanism).

- *Rest and Restore*—Do you often feel in a rush? Perhaps you grunted or laughed when you read that line? The human condition often feels like it's on some kind of a warp speed to nowhere. Maybe you've noticed that rushing doesn't make anything better. In fact, there's an overwhelming number of studies that detail the harms of stress—more than enough to let us know that if we don't rest and restore, our bodies will make us stop. One practice I've taken up recently is creating more space between everything I do (back to that all-important need to create space we talked about in Chapter 3). I don't want to be rushing around if I can avoid it. If you're feeling irritated or annoyed, chances are you're feeling rushed. Instead of lingering in that annoyance, I'm giving myself little breaks between meetings and chores. Downtime. And I'm better for it. However you rest and restore, make it a top priority. It's important. And your mental clarity and ability to avoid those little feelings of annoyance will improve. Make rest a priority, and everything else gets better too.

A NONVERBAL EXERCISE YOU CAN PRACTICE

Wonder Person Pose

Before a situation that feels a little stressful, try doing the Wonder Woman (I like to call it the Wonder Person). This exercise is great when you want a boost in confidence:

- Time yourself for two minutes.
- Stand up straight.
- Look straight ahead—look in a mirror if you want.
- Place your feet shoulder distance apart, with your toes facing slightly outward, but still comfortable.
- Put your hands on your hips.

Do you feel more open and expansive? Relaxed, ready to face whatever?

Psychologist and speaker Amy Cuddy says that studies show that if you stand like Wonder Woman (Person) for two minutes, you embrace risk and feel more self-assured (Cuddy 2012).

Listen, these types of poses help us open up and say "Yes, and" to ourselves and the world. While you're doing the Wonder Person, try observing yourself without thinking. That's right. Instead, focus your attention on the bold stance you see in the mirror, try different positions, and have fun. Get present and grounded. And playful.

While this is a pose you can practice on your own—even in the bathroom before an event—Ralph and I often add the power pose to our improv workshops, and we notice a difference right away. I think of our times with groups of university students. They often enter a room visibly shut down, closed off, and scrunching up their bodies like twisted pretzels. They're shy.

Nervous. Worried. Definitely lacking in confidence. They walk into our workshops, called Improv@Work, and they often have no idea what the working world is about. They're learning to communicate, and in their minds, communication in the working world is this fear-based thing where they have to either give in to whatever demands are placed upon them or overcompensate and try to take control by dominating. They're mirroring what they believe the adult world wants them to be. Our goal is to disrupt those tendencies.

There we are, Ralph and me, walking around a group of thirty students in Wonder Person pose, all standing in a circle. Everyone is upright, hands on hips, eyes gazing ahead—and they're all smiling, chuckling, laughing. A far cry from the frightened students who entered the room. They've been given permission to try something new. And they're embracing a new reality, one where everyone has the right to feel assured and free to try new things together.

Time and time again, nonverbal communication is something we employ to get everyone feeling strong, confident, present, and ready to take on the world. And it's something you can make part of your daily practice wherever you are. It's as easy as noticing how you are standing, how your body is positioned, and how your nonverbal cues appear to yourself and other people.

Our Individual Self-Awareness

When we walk into the office or log on to a virtual call, we are all human beings participating in our worlds as the individuals we have become. Yet do we consider how we've become who we are? Some call it a combination of nature and nurture, and this is undoubtedly true. We are born into a certain body with all its billions of cells, its preconditions, and a unique brain that we get to develop. From there, we are deeply impacted by the places, people, and situations that influence our every moment. How do we honor the person we are, while also staying open to new experiences and new ideas? A sense of humor helps. And self-awareness. It's a practice, really. A lot of the effort around self-awareness comes through observation. We need to continuously keep in touch with our bodies and minds, ever present in observing our thoughts and feelings with awareness and empathy. Go easy on yourself. You're an evolving human being. At the same time, questioning what you've learned—sometimes unlearning—and staying present with your in-the-moment lived experiences becomes part of that moment-by-moment practice. And improv is a part of it all. After all, isn't life an improvisation?

How Improv and "Yes, And" Help Our Individual Practice

Improv techniques and "Yes, and–ing" your personal life can bring about surprisingly meaningful changes—whole new ways of engaging with yourself and those around you. Consider these benefits:

Listening

Improv helps stop the "chatterbox" of your brain. You must listen when you improvise with other people. If you don't, you will quickly lose the momentum of the exercise. And when you begin to listen with intention, you will find yourself listening more effectively.

Confidence

As you've seen in earlier chapters, improv teaches that failure is okay. Even necessary. Important for growth. Once you accept that failing is good—the sky's the limit. Improv is a great way to learn to fail through fun. You'll be happily laughing all the way to your more confident self.

Trust

When you improvise, you learn to build authentic, trusting relationships. You share risks that let you bond through co-creation and play. This practice extends into your relationship with yourself. You start observing yourself and gaining self-awareness, which helps you be more present. When you stay in the moment, you respond with more clarity and a greater ease. Better people skills emerge.

Flexibility

You will get in touch with your "blind spots"—those areas of your psyche where you lack clarity or awareness. You know, the places where you are not so open, or are maybe trying to control things. Improv gets you out of control mode and into collaboration mode.

Nonverbal Communication

Improv, again through observation, will show you where you're giving your power away. Maybe your posture, your voice, or a shrugging of your shoulders is telling other people that you don't really believe in your ideas. Nonverbal awareness helps create a more composed you as well.

"Thinking on Your Feet"

The more you engage in improv, the more you will train your brain to respond quickly. It's exercise for the brain. Stronger reflexes and well-honed reaction skills will emerge. Improv will help ground you and prepare you to listen and respond with greater ease. Again, improv is a low-stakes way to help you prepare for high-stakes events.

Creativity

You may believe you are creative, or you may believe you are not creative. Truth is, we are all creative—we simply need to tap into that capacity. Improv gets you there. If you already have a robust relationship with your artistic side, improv will expand your inventiveness. If you are a little shy in this area, improv will open you up to your visionary possibilities.

Bonus Skill! Mind Reading

Okay, not really mind reading—and yet, sort of like mind reading. Through improv, you will begin to innately observe other people's verbal and nonverbal communication, and respond with more fluidity. Since improv helps with the mental state of flow, your decision-making skills become more spontaneous. You can quickly assess a situation, let go of judgment and overthinking, and open to greater self-expression and sharing. You move from fear to expansion. Now, you're letting go of the old scripts and inherited ideas, and making space for discovery. Through this process of inviting in openness, you leave room to get more curious about people. Suddenly, you are truly listening to people and gauging their real intentions, instead of making up stories about what they mean based on your own narratives. So, yes, now you are mind reading, because you're engaged in a place of understanding through awareness and observation.

It's an Inside Job

When you focus on how you function as an individual in your life, your self-awareness transfers to your working world. You'll notice yourself operating in ways that beautifully reflect your developing strengths. It's worth mentioning that improv also helps you become a highly present parent and a great listener who makes friends more easily. It improves your presentation and networking skills, deepens your emotional intelligence, and keeps you laughing and present. You overcome your fear of failure because you now truly understand that failure is a requirement for growth.

Of course, these individual skills are highly transferable to team bonding and leadership too. Everything connects. Let's dig deeper into explorations with improv that you can do on your own to build individual skills, and that will also help you support your team. Really, the list is endless. Here are a few exercises that you can easily bring into your daily practices and rituals.

Life Is an Improv

"Yes, and" yourself. Observe yourself throughout a day and count how many unexpected things happen. (You may want to keep a notepad on hand, or you will likely lose track pretty quickly.) As you walk down the street, you might see a friendly cat and have some kind of a reaction; a neighbor, who elicits a greeting from you; a bicycle whizzing by, which creates a thought . . . on and on. None of these little moments are planned. Yet, they are part of the everyday improv that makes up your life. You are improvising as you go throughout your day. Whether you are at home or the office, observe yourself as you interact with people. Watch as judgments of other people arise (all these judgments are based on our past experiences, which can only ever be limited and biased). As a judgment comes up, get curious. Ask yourself, "What is this?" Can you instead get curious about the other person or situation? Leave space for something new to emerge? An unexpected joy, a laugh, a shared human moment?

"Originality is unexplored territory. You get there by carrying a canoe—you can't take a taxi."

—Alan Alda

Always Observe the Ego

As we've been discussing, somewhere along the way, after years of experiences—big and small—we now have a collection of thoughts, and we draw on these past thoughts anytime something happens. So now, when you see a butterfly, you might recall some past experience with a butterfly or think about that time when you visited the butterfly conservatory. Or, when you see your coworker, you recall past interactions with them, and you are influenced by all those recalled moments, creating an impression. And due to the box of thoughts upon which all your opinions are now created, you may believe that whatever you think is right. This is your ego. We all have one, and we are all conditioned to think a certain way because of our past. The ego is extremely important to our survival (we wouldn't be able to function without it—the ego helps us make sense of the world around us and works hard to keep us safe). Yet the ego can also run amok (and frequently does), as it tells you to believe every thought you have. During improv training, I will sometimes say, "You don't have to believe all your thoughts." This is actually a deep spiritual teaching too, which helps us as individuals get into a habit of observation and awareness. It's where improv and personal spiritual practice meet.

More Awareness & Observation (Let's Make It a Habit)

Showing up as an aware individual really is a practice. It's a moment-by-moment practice of observing ourselves in situations and, instead of automatically listening to our box of thoughts, actively choosing to get inquisitive in the moment. We begin by asking ourselves: What new experience can we have in this moment? When I see that coworker, is it possible that I've judged that person based on a limited number of times I've seen them? Can I stay open? Get curious instead.

More on the Perplexing Ego

Consider this: each one of us carries within us an aspect of humanity—our unique frame of reference regarding what the world is and who we are within it.

As the writer, speaker, and philosopher Alan Watts said in 1966, "Every individual is a unique manifestation of the Whole, as every branch is a particular outreaching of the tree." Yet here we are, billions of people, each of us walking around with the certainty that we are right. That's you and that's me. It's all of us. To engage as open, actively listening, present human beings, we have to observe ourselves constantly. Meanwhile, our ego—that collection of stories—is always speaking up, a chatterbox full of opinions on every situation. And all these ideas about being right? They are entirely based on past assumptions.

If we listen only to the constant feedback from our thoughts—notes from the past telling us what is right, what to think, and how to be—we lose the ability to stay present, improvise, and play. We stagnate. Our bias keeps us in an ever-narrowing place. Our minds control us, sometimes in unhealthy ways. And we lose the ability to direct our minds.

Yet our ego, that box of thoughts, plays a critical role. Without it, we'd all be running around haphazardly, doing ridiculous things. (Come to think of it, some of us still are.) So, our egos are both a hindrance and a help. Geez—how do we make sense of that?

Evolution brought us to this paradox, this juxtaposition. Along the way, we started thinking, speaking, writing, and creating. It's mind-blowing, really. Then we started overthinking, completely identifying with our thoughts. We got totally caught up in the messages from our parents, educators, and peers—some good, some bad, yet typically a mixed bag. We absorbed them. And that swirl of thoughts took hold of our ability to see clearly, to behold each other in our gorgeousness, to apply tenderness to the situations that call for it.

It is becoming abundantly clear that learning to direct our minds, rather than letting our minds control us, is the way forward. As part of our practice, we find the things that are good for us, like meditation, communing with nature, stretching our bodies, and yes, improv.

So, we do the dance of liberating ourselves from the rigid grip of ego without losing our self-awareness. That tree, with its infinite branches, its vast network of roots and leaves, connects us to one another across the world and through time. We can rest on that truth. Or maybe we are part of a huge band of musicians creating every type of music, each of us representing an instrument—a note, like a songbird all of us linked in melody. We play and we listen. We move in and out of the spotlight. Sometimes we are silent, even—allowing another to shine. Giving and taking. Sharing our unique sounds.

While our egos strive to protect us with fixed perceptions, still we reach toward one another. You might say we are "Yes, and–ing" all the time.

"Yes, And–ing" Yourself

What kinds of practices help you to say "Yes, and" to yourself and open to your full potential? Or, let me rephrase that. I would say becoming your best self is a singular, lifelong practice. It's that moment-by-moment process of habit-shifting, getting out of your own head, and creating an experience of your world in the present moment.

The Building Blocks of All the Little Moments

Apply awareness to the way you spend your day. Whatever is happening, just observe it. Start to notice the little moments. Notice them and accept them. Acceptance is a way to listen to ourselves—hear our inner world speak up.

- What are you doing? Observe that.

- What are you saying? Observe that.

- Are you being reactive? Observe that.

- Do you feel good? Irritated? Joyful? Neutral? Angry? Observe it all.

- Accept it all.

This improvisational practice of observation and acceptance can give you insight into what you are searching for, interested in, and wondering about. When you embrace this moment-by-moment practice of staying present, you move beyond the trappings of the mind. And then, when thoughts pop up, you can get playful with them.

Through observing your thoughts and gaining some awareness, you start to create some space around your thinking mind. A magical opening appears. Time shifts. What is time, anyway, except another human construct? You shift. Then your reality shifts. After all, your outside world is always a reflection of your inside world. Accept whatever is happening in your present moment and love it. Stay high-vibe. There is nothing you can have in the material world that can ever replace your highest vibration state. That is your practice.

A great place to start shifting into presence, which is a place where we often begin in our improv workshops, is to focus on your breath. You can do this anywhere, anytime, because guess what? Breathing is your number one presence tool.

We start to breathe together when we operate as a team —a grounding practice.

Breathing—You know how, when you're on an airplane, the safety presentation always tells you that in the event of an emergency, you need to put your own oxygen mask on first before helping others, including any children you might have?

You want to put the metaphorical oxygen mask on yourself first too—in the form of deep care, self-love, and time spent being silly, playful, and fun, as well as, yes, doing meaningful work. This way, you will have the energy to show up for yourself, your loved ones, your profession, and your life. Put the oxygen mask on yourself first. Every time.

So, how are you showing up for the most important person in your life—you? In this moment?

Let's begin.

Breathe. Notice your breath. There are many breathing exercises to help relieve stress. When you observe your breath and breathe deeply, your brain gets the message to calm down and relax. So, if you're feeling anxious about something—a big event, the latest news, or you're about to step out onto a stage—attention to your breath can improve your state. Box breathing is one powerful method for creating calm and allowing yourself to reset.

Box breathing is a powerful and proven tool to combat anxiety and stress. Navy SEALs employ this technique during high-stress times (Nazish 2019). You can enlist this helpful method before a high-stress event, when you're feeling anxious, or anytime you want to reduce stress. Try these four steps to clear your mind and regain a feeling of calm before any event or presentation:

Box breathing has four basic steps, each lasting four seconds.

1. Breathe in for four seconds.
2. Hold the breath for four seconds.

3. Breathe out for four seconds.
4. Hold the breath for four seconds.

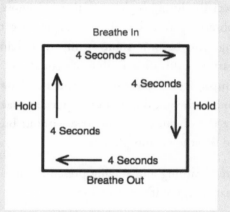

Your breath is like the ocean, moving inward and outward, always in motion. Imagine your breath as ocean waves. When you give it your attention, there is a change. Suddenly you are super present. Suddenly you are here, now.

What if you started your day with just one minute of this type of focus? Simple: you'd be setting yourself up to be present all day long. Plus, guess what? You can do this anytime during the day. What if you forgot to give your breath focus right when you woke up? You can do it in the shower, in the car (on your bike, if you're me), in your office, before bed—whenever. The important thing is that by observing your breath and giving it focus, you are creating space for yourself and giving the moment that you are in attention.

Why does this practice matter? We have a tendency to hold our breath, especially during high-stress times. I know I do. Once you start observing your breath, you begin to get away from overthinking, you become more firmly rooted in your body, and you start to cultivate a feeling of rootedness, which then positively impacts your encounters throughout the day. Paying attention to breathwork is the most important practice you can do. To state the obvious, we can't live without breathing, and yet we often breathe on autopilot.

While you're breathing and staying present, you can engage in another great energy shift: affirmations.

Affirmations

What if you had little phrases you said to yourself throughout the day that immediately changed your emotional state? I'm talking about a short sentence (or a few) that makes you feel better right away. In chapter 1, I talked about the "I'm grateful" exercise. Even though all you're doing is throwing your arms wide and saying "I'm grateful" for fourteen seconds, the activity has a deep impact on your brain's dopamine and serotonin neurotransmitters. Affirmation practices go a long way toward shifting your perceptions. Consider adopting or adapting some of the following ways of using language to activate your happiness chemicals.

Bending Is Good

An affirmation came to me one day when I kept dropping things and having to bend to pick them up. I was getting irritated and out of sorts. It came to me suddenly that every time I dropped something and bent down, I could say, "Bending is good."

And I've been saying that to myself ever since, every time I drop anything. I drop my pen. "Bending is good." I drop my phone. (Happens all the time. You too?) "Bending is good." I drop a mug. "Bending is good." And if I actually break something, I still say it. "Bending is good." Because guess what—bending *is* good. In so many ways. It's good for your body, your mind, and your spirit. It's good for your soul.

It's good for your relationships too. Ever watch trees in the wind? They bend and sway together. They're all different, moving gracefully, beautifully, and naturally. They don't judge each other, gossip, or put each other down. They cooperate. As the spiritual teacher Ram Dass, the author of the classic book *Be Here Now* said, "When you go out into the woods, and you look at trees, you see all these different trees. And some of them are bent, and some of them are straight, and some of them are evergreens, and some of them are whatever. And you look at the tree and you allow it . . . And so, I practice turning people into trees" (Dass 1971). I honor the diversity of humankind by bending like a tree.

Try out affirmations. Make them up. Change your state. Rewire your brain.

Life Is a Moment-by-Moment Practice

So, what does all of this have to do with becoming a "Yes, and" person and a conscious improvisational leader? Once we start saying yes to ourselves while doing all the little things, we open up to a new appreciation of life. This is the moment-by-moment practice we've been talking about. Does this mean you need to be perfect? *Noooooooooooo.* (There's another good use of that important word). Besides, what is perfect, anyway? Isn't it some preconditioned idea? Ego again. Isn't "perfect" different for everyone? And does "perfect" even exist? Actually, embracing your imperfections (if that's what they are) is a part of the moment-by-moment practice. Saying "Yes" to each moment is a part of this ever-flowing process. Having awareness and observing what is happening in each of your moments are key. Giving space. Breathing. Being conscious of your breath. Being present. Changing your state through affirmations. The moment-by-moment practice is your life unfolding right before you, in the exact moment you are in. Right now. Reading these words. That's it. The beauty of this practice is that all you need to do is surrender to the now.

Acceptance as a Pathway to Growth

Here's a practice: The next time you get a feeling—any feeling, like joy, anger, disgust, surprise, shame, envy, or fear—simply observe it without thinking. Accept it. If a thought tries to attach itself to your emotion, observe that too. Just let it be. Watch it. Pretty soon, it will dissolve. If you keep going with this practice, you'll get into the habit of observing your feelings. And you'll find that you're becoming less reactive in ways that aren't helpful to you.

People always want to know if this means they should never feel anything, or if they need to deny their feelings. Quite the opposite. Invite your feelings in. Feel them deeply. And hey, look, sometimes we have a dark night of the soul, and sometimes we need to stay there for a while—that happens in life too. What I can tell you with absolute assuredness is that if you start to practice the art of awareness, observation, and acceptance you will also experience greater presence (that lovely in-the-moment feeling of being truly here in the now). Of course, life will continue to present challenges—yet when it does, you will be better equipped to handle them.

Your Individual "Yes, And" Practice

We've talked about awareness, observation, acceptance, getting out of your conditioned mind, and ego. Guess what can help you practice these great clarifiers and move you away from judging, negativity, and other intolerant behaviors? Yes, improv. Here's a little-known secret: improv is actually a great spiritual practice. You see, improv, a nonconceptual practice, gets you away from concepts, conditionings, and other limiting belief systems. And it's fun. Laughter breaks through ego, as well as all those outdated stories rooted in conditioning. Humor is a wonderful clarifier that breaks through both ego and distractions.

As part of a group, I did an in-person program with the author and spiritual teacher Eckhart Tolle in 2019, in California, and I was struck by how closely his teachings align with everything I understand about improv. His main points are all about being in the moment, acceptance and surrendering to what is, moving from thinking to aware presence, and overcoming your ego and the conditioning of your mind. Improv is also about staying present in the moment, staying open to what is being offered, letting go of judgment and the need to be right, and observing ego. Both spiritual teachings and improv have a strong foundation in curiosity—a widening of the mind that stays open to different ideas. (As an aside, Tolle says that his single greatest achievement is being able to stop thinking whenever he wants—try that!) You might know him through his important book *The Power of Now* (1997). And I also like *Stillness Speaks* (2003), which I have handy and can flip open to any page to get a spirituality boost.

Now, put on your favorite album, and be with some music that you love. Consider how your team is like a band, and you can all make beautiful music together as you embark on the improv journey. This individual "Yes, and" experience—it's truly a moment-by-moment practice. Learning how to cultivate your inner world is key to becoming increasingly present with other people. It starts with you.

Chapter Summary

- "Yes, and" is also an individual practice, and you begin by "Yes, and–ing" yourself.
- Experiential improv exercises allow you to practice awareness and observation—making self-awareness a habit.
- Improv gets you out of your head (overthinking, conditioning, and ego) and into the present moment.
- Ego is a strange paradox! (We need ego, and yet ego can also run amok!)
- Life is a moment-by-moment practice through which you cultivate your inner world.
- When you pay attention to your inner world, you are more present with people, and your outer world reflects back to you a greater sense of ease.

CHAPTER SIX

How to Be a "Yes, And" Leader

*The test of a first-rate intelligence is the
ability to hold two opposed ideas in the mind at the
same time and still retain the ability to function.*

—F. Scott Fitzgerald

It's 1997, and I'm associate director of communications for
a large telecommunications company. Over the past decade,
this company has experienced many business shifts, and I've
made some lifelong friendships too—absolutely the result of
deep personal and professional connection. As the company
went from being a monopoly to adapting to a competitive
environment to launching a little product called the internet,
there was a lot of flux. There was some pretty good training too,
including something called "Strategy of the Dolphin," where
I was invited to map out the highs and lows of my life, and
discover whether I'm like a shark or a dolphin. (A dolphin is
"flexible, responsive, accepting"—yep, that sounds good).

The course, which was a series of sessions over a few months, was
meant to help people access their adaptable, creative side during
times of change. It was highly improvisational. I remember that
we all had to stand in a part of the room that represented our
brain style (based on answers to a questionnaire), and I was
a predominate right brain, according to the tests. As I've said

throughout this book, we need all types of brains—that's what makes the world go round. This training stayed with me, and it still stays with me today. My phrase from chapter 1, paragraph two, of this book about how to deal with a challenging situation comes from my memory of this training: "Give in, get out, or try for a breakthrough" (Lynch and Kordis 1990). Training can be memorable, and it can change your life.

Recently, Ralph and I were training a team of about forty insurance company team members on communication and "Yes, and" philosophies for the workplace, and after the event, one of the longest-term employees said to me, "That was the best training I've had in fifty years at this company." Wow. Hearing that kind of comment makes my whole heart happy. Why can training resonate so deeply? It's because certain types of training get us out of our regular routine and open the brain to another way of being. At times, it's a matter of convergent vs. divergent thinking. What's the difference, you ask? Well, convergent thinking—a more logical approach to problemsolving—is when you apply one clear-cut solution to a problem, such as when you answer a multiple-choice test, or when you know there is one possible outcome in a given situation. Divergent thinking—which is where you would typically apply improv skills—is a thought process or method you would employ to explore many possible solutions. Divergent thinking is great for brainstorming, for example, when you want to be spontaneous and allow many creative ideas to spring forth.

What does all this mean for you? As a leader, you might first encourage your team to apply divergent thinking to a situation—to invite innovation and creativity so that many ideas are considered as potential solutions to a challenge. Then, after you've accepted all the ideas that you possibly can, you might apply convergent thinking, so you can problem-solve and narrow your many ideas down to one or two. So, divergent thinking is where improv training comes in. You hold a brainstorming session with a focus on divergent thinking (all ideas are good ideas when you're brainstorming), and you follow that session up with a session where you narrow down the ideas and put in place a "next steps" process (convergent thinking).

When your brain experiences this switch, from mainly thinking in a convergent way (and limiting yourself quickly to one solution) to applying divergent thinking (and coming up with as many ideas as possible to access peak creativity), it has a profound and enduring impact. As we've been discussing, improv is wonderful for creating this type of lasting impression. Research clearly supports this fact. More and more scientific articles show that "improv experience promotes divergent thinking, uncertainty tolerance, and affective well-being" (Felsman 2020). When you're making decisions, brainstorming, or trying new ideas, you want to go back and forth between divergent and convergent thinking. Oftentimes, convergent thinking is the focus, and not a lot of time is spent on the divergent skill. As a result, you don't take the time to get creative and come up with all the ideas that you can. And the more ideas you generate, the better—that's how you come up with the really great ideas. You want to make space for both kinds of thinking.

Divergent Thinking—Questioning (Ideas)

Creative, Horizontal Thinking

- Creative Process—Saying "Yes, and" to ideas.

- Brainstorming Time—All ideas are good ideas, and every idea is encouraged. (Remember: an idea can spark another idea—and the more ideas, the better your chances of getting to a great idea.)

- Generate as Many Ideas as Possible—And stay open to possibility.

Convergent Thinking—Answering (Facts)

Critical, Vertical, Analytical Thinking

- Apply judgment.

- Sort through ideas and narrow your focus.

- Be Selective—This is the time to make choices and decisions (act on the top one to three ideas).

When you think about it, how often do you willfully apply the principles of divergent and convergent thinking to your planning processes? You need the two working together—like yin and yang. It's always back to that balancing act. It's also good to separate the process of brainstorming from the process of applying judgment to your ideas, because they do rely on different approaches. You'll notice that one type of thinking can be more frustrating for some people, while others find that type of thinking very easy—it's another type that gives them trouble. It's back to having different brains at work. In his great, short book *Creativity,* John Cleese enlists a number of writers and educators to discuss the importance of play in accessing creativity. Cleese talks about a creativity study conducted by psychologist Donald MacKinnon, who actually focused his study on architects. The findings showed that when architects "become really curious about it for its own sake . . . not trying to avoid making mistakes," that's when they had the strongest and most creative results. Through playfulness (Cleese 2020). That's improv. As a leader, you can invite your team to experience divergent thinking through improv in order to give them that positive brain boost, which bonds people together and builds trust, while also benefiting their whole communication, creativity, and planning process.

> "When we're trying to be creative, there's a real lack of clarity during most of the process . . . when you first have a new idea, you don't get critical too soon."
>
> —John Cleese

To Improv or Not to Improv

Earlier, I mentioned that I've led a lot of improv workshops and trainings where the team leader said, "I don't need to be at this improv training, right, it's my team that needs this?" Unless this training is particular to the team's goals, you will want to be there. It's critical, actually. Does a conductor directly engage with the orchestra? Do musicians vibe off of one another, rehearsing, to create beautiful music? Do leaders and teams need to come together to create synergy and flow? What can happen is a leader starts to believe they are separate from their team—superior, even. Nothing could be further from the truth. While it is true that everyone has been hired to do a particular job, every single person has an equal importance and responsibility for making a team function. Everything links together. If a link is missing, the whole chain weakens—breaks. Just like a band, the team needs consistent communication between all members. You want to be a part of the improv magic. You need to be. It's about respect too. Plus your credibility as the team leader. People need and deserve to be respected for the role that they play.

If you think your team is not working together effectively, the first place to look is at yourself. Now, I'm not saying that you have a perfect team and you're imperfect, or vice versa. I am saying that if one of your team members is not functioning well, has emotional issues, or isn't engaged, then they need help. Support. So, as the leader, you need to put in place the right training and development systems to make sure your team feels seen and heard. You've all got to have each other's back. (That fundamental of improv.) Often, a collaboration with human resources or your training department helps in this area. We're all people (evolving human beings), so everyone needs help sometimes. You too.

So, how can "Yes, and" help a team stay on course—feel championed? And how can "Yes, and" build that all-important team trust all along the way? On so many levels. It's no secret that people want to be acknowledged and that recognition is at the top of your list when it comes to leading a team. "I hear you. I'm listening. Let's 'Yes, and' this!"

The Magic of Listening

Picture a great saxophone player playing beautiful notes. Yet the conductor keeps throwing little pebbles into his horn. At first, the sax player keeps playing (although the sound is already distorted). Yet, as more and more pebbles get added to the mix, the sax player finally gives up, throws the instrument to the ground, and lies down, burned out. Unable to play.

Leaders sometimes don't listen well or don't fully understand what their team members are doing. And so, they keep adding more and more responsiblity, mostly connected to growing revenue expectations. They fill their team's horns with pebbles until they've demoralized and exhausted the people who most deserve to be listened to.

That's our world. Burned out from this more-more-more. And what happens? The outcome is less-less-less. Because burned out people can't function. They stop doing anything. Rightfully so. Does this impact your revenue? Yes-yes-yes!

This disconnect between leaders and teams is something I've witnessed time and time again—both as a team member and as a team leader. As one example, I was a consultant for many years, hired to coach and train sales and marketing teams. You may know that sales and marketing sometimes experience conflict (okay, more than sometimes, often). It's simply because different types of brains are at work—both needed and both trying to achieve different goals. On the one hand, a team of sales managers is responsible for selling, and on the other hand, you have a team of marketing managers developing and promoting the brand. This scenario is meant to be collaborative, yet sometimes the teams can be at odds. They don't wholly understand one another due to their different roles. And, even though the leaders of both teams want synergy between the players, the communication often isn't flowing. Here are some of the challenges I've seen:

- The sales leaders didn't believe that marketing understood sales, and since marketing didn't contribute directly to revenue, they thought it was less important.

- The marketing leaders thought the salespeople were high maintenance and that sales was in a rush, instead of carefully considering best practices on how to communicate with customers.

- There were no consistent processes in place, causing dysfunction, because everyone just did what they wanted. This led to a lack of effective planning and implementation of either team's desired approaches.

- There was little time for effective conversation—or active listening—because the company was in high-growth mode. The company was always talking about what dollars were coming in instead of focusing on customer needs, putting their people first, and effective processes (revenue will also happen if you focus on people first—this is a concept still lost on many companies).

Working with these companies was always interesting, because many of the leaders were super smart, thoughtful, and competent. And yet, there was frequently a complete disconnect between sales and marketing. Because marketing has the goal of generating awareness of a company and its products and services, while sales wants to turn that awareness into a purchase, they tend to compete rather than collaborate. Ideas and ways of communicating are not passed on because no one is truly listening—egos get in the way. Everyone rushes around in a state of chaos, when it would better serve everyone to adopt clearly defined roles and apply unity toward their common goal of reaching customers.

This scenario plays out over and over and over—almost everywhere I've been. It all goes back to this imbalance of yang (fast, profits) over yin (building trust, nurturing the team). Instead, what happens is that teams get so toxic—so unable to communicate at all—that revenue is finally impacted. And that's when the senior leaders take note. Suddenly, it becomes important to uncover all the reasons why profits are dropping.

Here are some approaches to address the psyches of different teams, instead of waiting until there's a crisis:

- Build an effective partnership/relationship between departments—establishing common ground and a "we're in it together" mentality.

- Focus on long- and short-term plans that consistently prioritize effective communication between all stakeholders, sections, leaders, and teams.

- Share between all team members to bring best practices to the whole team—and to keep that dialogue going, because best practices are always evolving (think regular brainstorming and ideation sessions).

- Plan to include constant internal and external training to help expand skills, connection, and a collaboration mindset, as well as to build trust.

- Offer a balanced, playful approach to working that takes into consideration each person's unique style of working, as well as their personal lives.

- Invite convergent and divergent brainstorming techniques into your company, and ground your planning process in creative practices that support your growth.

The 2023 Workplace Learning Report published by LinkedIn says that "building the agile future" means that learning and development "puts people and skills at the center of organizational success."

Top four focus areas for learning and development for 2023:

1. Aligning learning programs with business goals
2. Upskilling employees
3. Creating a culture of learning
4. Improving employee retention

What human skills matter the most, according to LinkedIn? (1) Management, (2) Communication, (3) Customer Service, and (4) Leadership.

How Can Leaders Create a Stronger L&D Strategy?

Whether the challenge is that people aren't getting along, people aren't speaking up, listening skills need to be improved, or confidence needs to grow, the way to improve L&D is to identify the key stressors and then create strategies to address those obstacles. Since obstacles are opportunities for growth, you can map out a plan that progresses as needs change. A living, breathing, revisable approach.

Effective skills development isn't something you achieve at one workshop—it's part of a consistent, progressing commitment to the growth of your team. And evolving you is part of the program. As an example, everyone needs to practice effective communication skills—all the time. As you plan your overall team strategy, make improv a regular part of your programs.

And, more directly, leaders and teams of all companies and organizations want to bring in experiential investigation to help people learn. When you are building your strategic plans for the year—your quarterly objectives, your monthly goals, your daily cadences—you always want to include your people development plans. You want to consider different ways to inspire, motivate, teach, train, and help people grow. Sprinkle your plans with improv training. Add in that experiential "get it in our hearts and bodies" approach that can be a catalyst for profound transformation.

How? "Yes, and" and the experiential improv exercises that help open you and your team to new ways of being. When we "Yes, and" each other, we say, "I am listening to you, I am hearing you, and even if we don't agree, we can come from a place of learning about one another." For leaders and teams, "Yes, and" helps everyone collaborate, as we've discussed, and it is particularly powerful for brainstorming and ideation. For developing creativity, which leads to innovation. On the human level, which is maybe the most important level when communication problems are serious, "Yes, and" lets people know their voices are heard.

How Does Improv Create Psychological Safety and New Team Dynamics?

First things first. As a leader, you need to slow down to speed up. It may sound counterintuitive, yet it's true. Slow down, listen to your team without seeking a quick fix, and put into place the support, planning, and processes that will help. Listening is one of your top leadership skills. Let me say that again: Listening is one of your top leadership skills. Emblazon those words into your leadership tool kit: "Listening is one of my top leadership skills."

Bring in some external trainers, because they add an objective eye to the situation. Sit down with those trainers, talk about your team's challenges (and make sure you ask your team for input), and come up with an approach that supports your business and people objectives. In every chapter of this book, I talk about developing listening skills, because they're so important. To create psychological safety as a leader, you want to start with listening, brainstorming, and planning as a team— together. People need to be heard.

Let's say that your business and people objectives are to plan for the coming year, or create a new sales process, or link marketing and sales activities . . . probably all three of those areas are part of your agenda on a regular basis, and much more besides. To prepare for these planning sessions, your task is to open up communication. Shift the way your team feels about sharing ideas and getting creative. Invite everyone to speak up, be heard, give and receive, and fail and try again. You are opening up a safe space for creativity to emerge.

Build on this. Offer regular and frequent communication sessions, and practice what you preach. Let your team know you're not afraid to mess up, be confused, or expose your vulnerability. I've noticed time and time again that when leaders say, "I got that point wrong," or "I made a mistake," they become more relatable. Your credibility actually expands. Your courage to be genuine translates into your team's invitation to reveal their own realness. Together, trusting in one another's support, you can elevate the work you do and the joy with which you do it.

Exercise: Building Common Ground

When you are looking for ways to help cross-functional teams mesh together in productive and collaborative ways, it often comes down to building relationships. When you think about the people you've connected with over the years—the ones that stuck—wasn't some kind of personal connection at the heart of your bond? When I consider how sales and marketing, for example, can find common ground and build that trust, I can explore many improv exercises that really do help make that feeling of kinship emerge.

This next exercise is one that I've seen really transform team relationships. I've been in the room and can testify that when people are stretching their comfort zones together, all the while laughing and relating, something sticks. Keep in mind this exercise is simply here to review—that taste test I mentioned in chapter 1. It's a completely different experience when everyone is standing on their feet, with a helpful facilitator guiding the way, leading a team toward a bold new vision.

Ad Campaign

Each team stands in a semicircle, with four to six people per group for this exercise. These groups can have a mix of different participants, such as mixing people from marketing, sales, and customer support.

Facilitator leads by telling the group they will create an ad campaign, focusing on the invention of a brand-new product.

The one guideline is that everyone will enthusiastically say "Yes, and" to all ideas.

Steps

1. Invite everyone to shout out the fictional name of a brand-new invention. Facilitator selects the one that feels the most spontaneous, real, and interesting. Ideas do not need to be relevant to the company; however, they may be. Could be anything from diamond-encrusted lampshades to black and white triangular picture frames—anything goes. All ideas receive wonderful applause and everyone's idea is accepted as interesting.

2. Once the invention has been chosen, invite people to name the product.

3. Continue with wild applause throughout the activity. Facilitator selects the name.

4. Invite someone to select the target audience. It may be anything from butterflies to rock stars to kittens.

5. Next step is to invite a team to design a fifteen-second commercial.

6. Continue applause regardless of how crazy or outlandish the ideas may be (the crazier the better).

7. Invite them to cast a celebrity spokesperson.

8. Applause.

9. Then, invite someone to sing the jingle for the product (made up on the spot).

10. Applause.

11. Let the team know it's now time to release the final product to market, and finish with more wild and crazy applause.

Sounds fun, right?

It is fun, and there is a whole lot of learning going on too.

At the heart, this is an exercise that helps a team suspend judgment. Say "Yes, and" and support each other with joy and enthusiasm. It builds trust. Collaboration. Everyone is important and every idea has a place. When you are stepping outside your comfort zone while having a laugh, it doesn't even feel like you are uncomfortable. Especially since there are no mistakes—only acknowledgment. This exercise sets your team up for a wonderful relationship. Once you improvise together, you see one another differently—as human beings. And permission to fail is like a wish granted that forever changes the shape and scope of communication. And, of course, it's all about listening to each other with acceptance.

I've seen Ad Campaign shift the entire dynamics of a team on the spot. What makes this type of exercise so valuable to a team? It's because, often for the first time, they are allowed to be totally free with their ideas—and the leader (who is participating with the team, of course) is a part of this place in time where the team has permission to fail and be totally open to creativity. You know the saying: The magic happens on the other side of your comfort zone. It's true. People are always laughing, smiling, getting excited, speaking up, and opening up when they do this exercise, led by an experienced facilitator. The facilitator creates the environment for the team to experience something new. And the participation of the leader shows the team an openness they have never seen in their leader before. Over time, through more and more demonstrations of openness by the leader, the entire team shifts into a responsive jazz band, building on the sweet notes of the other players.

There's plenty of research to demonstrate how improv helps teams reach this musical flow state. A famous 2008 study by neuroscientist Charles Limb, where he conducted brain scans on musicians while they were improvising, shows how improv impacted people's brain activity. The bottom line: Improv gets you "in the zone," because the part of the brain that is like your inner critic (the dorsolateral prefrontal cortex) decreases in activity, and the part of your brain that accesses creativity (the medial prefrontal cortex) increases.

When I attended the 2023 Applied Improvisation Network Conference in Vancouver, improviser extraordinaire Colin Mochrie, of *Whose Line Is It Anyway?* fame, was there. (Yes, hilarious and adorable as always.) In front of about two hundred applied improvisers from around the world, he talked about Limb's study and how he had also been a test subject. The findings were the same, whether on musicians or on comedy performers who improvised—improv lets you access a part of your brain that focuses your attention, suspends judgment, and expands creativity. That's a great place to be when you want to innovate.

"Yes, And" as a Part of Regular Brainstorming Sessions and Team Meetings

Want to create team flow and keep elevating the level of trust, acceptance, and respect for each other? Make brainstorming a regular part of the schedule. Weekly, monthly, quarterly—whatever. Let the team decide. Talk about it together. That's how you get buy-in. It's not about dictating an approach—bring the team into your decision-making process. Create a safe space for the team to have their say. And listen. For each session, you can have a different leader. You can either bring someone in to facilitate, so that you have an objective person around, or you can do it yourselves. Whatever works. Maybe you have a white board (which you can have in person or online), and every idea is captured and shared with the team following the meeting. From these sessions, you can create action items, and also agree as a team when an idea has had its day and needs to go. Improv and the power of "Yes, and" can help a group stay on track and avoid letting certain people speak too much while other people speak too little. Improv helps make a good team great. There's that balance thing again—a continuous process of open communication that leads to trust.

Shh!

A while back, I was reading the book *Persuasion*, by Canadian business leader and Dragon's Den alumnus Arlene Dickinson. I was reading her chapter "Shh!" and it starts by saying, "I used to have a sign on my desk that summed up, in a single word, a little-known secret to success in business (and in life, for that matter). A lot of people coming into my office for the first time did a double take when they saw that sign, which is how I knew it was an exotic and mysterious piece of advice. Here's what it said: 'Listen.'" (2011). When I read that, I'm pretty sure I shouted out loud, "Yes!" Because listening is the primary active ingredient in improv, and so important to leadership—and life—that it can't be overemphasized. Again, we are applying the rule of balance here. So many people are caught up in their thinking minds while they are listening to other people. I do it too. We all have to apply these fundamental rules of awareness and observation while engaged in conversation. What we want to do is listen to understand, not simply to respond with our own story. We want to listen without thinking. (I know I keep saying this. It's because repetition is a key component of learning. The brain forms new pathways when it hears repeated messages, and absorbs information better). My business partner, Ralph, often says in workshops, right before we do an active listening exercise, "We're going to do an exercise where you will listen to the other person until they are completely finished. While you are listening, you might have this better, more interesting, story about yourself pop up. Try to observe that, and let it go. Your goal here is to listen completely, and you will become so popular, and no one will know why they like you so much. It's because you listen."

Last Word Response

One of my personal favorite listening exercises is called Last Word Response. It's a beautiful exercise for helping people experience the art of listening without waiting to respond with their own story. This activity creates that all-important component called "presence" and keeps everyone in the moment, which is really one of the deep secrets of life. In fact, what I would add as the real benefit of listening is that listening creates understanding—it provokes people to pay attention to the space flowing around and between all your words. It's the space that matters, which is where the magic happens.

With this exercise, you have two people facing each other. One person says a short line, and the second person starts their sentence with the last word that was said.

Here's how it can go:

> Person A: There is a beautiful sunset on the horizon.
>
> Person B: Horizon is a beautiful sight to behold.
>
> Person A: Behold this mighty pen, as I am about to write.
>
> Person B: Write in order to get things out of your mind and onto paper.
>
> Person A: Paper has so many lovely textures and offers an important way to communicate.

And so on.

It doesn't really matter if you get your sentence structure right, and it's not important if the conversation makes sense.

(Sometimes people say the exchange was all gobbledygook and sometimes they say they actually had a coherent conversation). The opportunity here is to start actively listening. Last Word Response prompts you to listen to another person, fully, without also thinking about how you are going to respond. That is the real point—and the true gift—of this exercise. You can't think about your response in advance because you don't know in advance what you can respond with. You must fully tune in to the exercise to make it work.

If you're wondering about whether or not listening is considered a "must have" skill in today's working world, yes, it really is. Our valued partner Great Place To Work thinks so too. During a 2023 webinar, CEO Michael C. Bush presented this topic and called it the most important slide in the deck: 9 High-Trust Leadership Behaviors that focus on listening:

© Great Place to Work

The Leadership Moment-by-Moment Practice

Okay, so you have a solid, continuous, and open communication practice going on with your team. And you're bringing your individual improv and presence practices to life situations everywhere you go—that moment-by-moment practice. The observation and awareness techniques we talked about in the last chapter remain central wherever you are.

Awareness and Observation—Your self-awareness as an individual—and a leader—is absolutely key. What are your biases? Your team will mirror you—your empathy, honesty, confidence, energy, and approach. You are being watched. Yet this doesn't mean you need to be superhuman or perfect—quite the opposite. In fact, true awareness comes from emotional intelligence. Improv helps too—gets you in touch with your playful, empathetic, human, open, spontaneous side.

What is happening in this moment that you're in? How are you feeling and what are you translating to other people through tone, movement, and verbal and nonverbal communication? The vibe you show up with every day—hour to hour, minute by minute—changes the state of your team. Yes, you're all in it together, yet the team looks to you, even as they also look to one another. As you develop your big-picture strategies—your learning and development programs, including your team communication, brainstorming, and innovation practices—you are also always keeping in touch with your inner world. Yes, it's a juggling act. The macro and the micro. You are constantly revisiting and revising your inner and outer worlds so you can lead with integrity, agility, and grace.

Chapter Summary

- Convergent and Divergent thinking—you need both to make quality decisions.

- A question: Do you—as a leader—need to participate in improv training? Yes! And!! (With a caveat—those times when your team will benefit from peer group exercises specifically.)

- Another question: What is your top skill needed for leadership development? (Hint: You will know this answer if you read the chapter.)

- And a third: As the conductor of your team, are you creating a balance of "yin and yang" musical goodness? Hint: When in balance, a team has flow and a feeling of flourishing (like a pleasing alliteration sound). And, the research bears it out.

- Putting it all together: As a leader, when you focus on the well-being of your team—through effective communication skills training, caring about their health and wellness, and modeling "having each other's back"—your team will thrive, leading to happy customers, and the natural by-product will be increased revenue. Putting revenue first is not a viable long-term solution, and research supports this fact.

- Practicing self-awareness is a leadership skill. Improv can help.

- And finally, *Listen. Listen. Listen.* "Yes, and" helps you practice the art of true listening—a super skill.

CHAPTER SEVEN

The "Yes, And" Company Evolution

*One of the things we've learned in all our research is
that it all begins with people.*

—JIM COLLINS

P icture this: Five of us are on stage. This is our second time
working with this large, international software company.
We've been invited two years in a row to improv train their
hundred and fifty senior leaders, who have flown in from all
over the world for a four-day retreat. They are here to share
knowledge and decide on annual plans, company direction, and
yes, company culture. We've been brought in as the lead-in to
their company-wide annual planning event.

We're doing "The Wave." You know, that fun sporting event
activity where everybody stands, yells, and raises their arms
up and down in unison. We're creating rhythm between all
the leaders, like a harmonious metachronal wave—helping
everyone bond, have fun, and get playful. We're establishing
a team dynamic. After a few more ice-melters, everyone is in
an elevated mood—we've increased the flow of those essential
endorphins that are behind the well-known therapeutic benefits
of laughter. Building connection.

Five of our best improv facilitators are opening the event, and
pretty soon we're all going to move into breakout rooms. Each

facilitator will work closely with a group of twenty to twenty-five individuals, getting everyone collaborating and building trust. Many people at this event have never met, and they represent diverse cultures, languages, identities, and backgrounds from across the globe. At the heart of it, these people are all present to connect and feel something together. Our job is to unify them and contribute to that company culture.

> Wondering about the benefits of laughter in the office? Research shows that teams that laugh together are more productive, less stressed, more collaborative, and more creative. Your brain gets more oxygen, causing the release of happy endorphins, and engagement improves (Heggie 2018).

In the breakout rooms, we're doing Clap Focus, a standard improv starter. Everyone is standing comfortably in a circle as the facilitator demonstrates. Stepping forward, their body movement and eye contact both directed at a specific individual across the circle, they bring their hands together and send a clap to that person with energy and commitment. Sounds simple. The other person receives this clap focus and sends it to another participant. At first, everyone's a little tentative. Self-conscious. Pretty soon, though, everyone is laughing and clapping, and as the focus shifts from person to person, everyone is engaged, alert, and ready—because you never know when you will be selected as the next one to receive that clap focus energy. This is another seemingly easy exercise that requires total presence, strong body language, eye contact, commitment, and dedication. You can't be anywhere else when you're doing improv. Clap focus begins to create this energy flow. Grounding everyone in presence. Suddenly the room is filled with positive chatter and movement, and everyone is collaborating. This deep work arises from what appear to be quite elementary activities. And we're just warming up. These icemelters are carefully designed to help adults play together and connect in new ways. These new bonds, emerging between this international group of leaders will contribute to a new and improved company culture. We're helping create a sense of community and belonging—camaraderie—before they begin their all-important planning sessions.

Company culture is critical. I was reading a 2021 *Harvard Business Review* article, "How to Lead in the Stakeholder Era," after the world had started to open up again. The author said "focus on purpose and people. The profits will follow" (Hubert 2021). While this certainly rings true, I've been watching this shift happen for years. When I think back to that 1980s young professional, working for a large publishing company, I have little memory of senior management engaging with employees. It definitely felt like a top-down, hierarchical approach. What was already happening, though, was that individual teams were creating their own blend of employee engagement—and those teams flourished. I recall weekly status report meetings where everyone would start off the week connecting and jamming on what was coming up, how everyone needed to work together to make projects flow. At first, people weren't that enthused about these meetings, and then they started looking forward to them. Connection. Shared sense of purpose.

My learned experience is that, over the years, the people-first approach arose because of individual intervention. Someone stepped up to make it happen. People encouraged owners and leaders to listen, because this top-down thing—it just wasn't working. It all comes down to listening—and that's improv. People improvised in their new working environment naturally. We're human beings, working things out all the time. That give and receive—ebb and flow. Yes, the stakeholder era is here, and it's been on the horizon for a while. Now, we're giving it voice and talking about it. Yet, it emerged through communication between people across all levels in companies—complex human beings with a full range of emotions and needs—making it happen. So if, as this article suggests, companies are now serving all stakeholders—employees, customers, suppliers, communities, and beyond—and "business and society cannot thrive if employees, customers, and communities are not healthy," then what can companies do to support this "common good" that provides for "the humanity of all stakeholders"?

Back to the improv workshop with the large international software company. Each of the improv facilitators is slightly customizing the workshop on the fly depending on how the group responds, because the nature of improv is that it's experiential. We listen to the input of participants as we train, watching how people are reacting to each exercise and what they need. Sometimes a group energy is slow to get moving—other times it's quick. We all have an outline we can reference, and we use that outline as a guide, adapting the exercises as we go. We are comfortable with all that because we're in the moment and we roll with what's happening—what the team is revealing about what they need.

At some point during this workshop, each of us will lead this foundational improv exercise: "No," "Yes, But," and "Yes, And."

Bring yourself into this scene.

The five facilitators, in their separate breakout rooms, move their group into a circle. Each facilitator leads this key exercise, stopping and starting things as the exercise progresses, in order to discuss how word choices, verbal enunciation, and body language contribute to how a group effectively communicates. This exercise is wonderful for the development of overall communication skills and holds a particular magic when helping a team get ready for brainstorming, ideation, and the planning process.

For the purpose of demonstration, we'll show this exercise conducted with just three people. In a live situation, we could have anywhere from two to twenty-five people participating. And for large groups, we would invite volunteers to the front of the room to demonstrate (led by our facilitator) so the whole group can watch. You will see that I'm employing a fictional example rather than a real-world business case. You can go either way depending on the circumstance. Sometimes a fictional example takes the pressure off your real-world situation and helps everyone stay objective. Why don't you play along as we do the exercise?

"NO," "YES, BUT," AND "YES, AND"

To start, we're going to make up a story. We have three fictional people who are saying one line each. For this story, after we introduce a topic in the first sentence, we will then use the word "No" before each line. Here's an example:

First person: Janie was an astronaut and it was her day off.

Second person: *No*, Janie was a dog walker and she was at the park.

Third person: *No*, Janie was watching television and eating potato chips.

First person: *No*, Janie loved knitting and she was at a class for mitten making.

Second person: *No*, Janie was reading a book.

Third person: *No*, Janie was a DJ at a night club, and she was spinning some tunes.

Now you try it—you can be all three people. While you are doing this exercise, take note of how you feel—jot down what comes up and what you notice about these interactions as you start your sentences with the word "No." (First you will create the opening sentence—see above example.)

First person: [Insert any first sentence that comes to mind.]

Second person: *No* . . . [Add what pops up for you without thinking too much.]

Third person: *No* . . .

First person: *No* . . .

Second person: *No* . . .

Third person: *No* . . .

All right, so how did it feel to hear "No" over and over? What did you learn about Janie? Did this scene progress? Was there any movement forward? (During live training, we have a little back-and-forth as a larger group, for one to two minutes, as we debrief on the outcomes of creating this scene when starting sentences with the word "No." And we always get some interesting answers from the group—everyone learns from each other.)

We also always talk about the word "No" and what it means. We speak to its value in certain situations—how "No" is super important when you want or need to put a stop to something. However, as the exercise reveals, "No" may not be the best choice when you are working together on a project, listening to your team members, and sharing ideas. The word "No" shuts down the flow of ideas, and nothing progresses at all—the story doesn't make any sense. Same goes for the planning process. A lot of "No" doesn't get you anywhere. Ideas do not move forward.

What if leaders just kept saying "No" every time a member of their team spoke up? (Remember our toxic leader from chapter 4?) "No" doesn't go a long way toward creating a people- and purpose-first company.

Let's try this exercise again, and this time we will start with the words "Yes, but . . ."

First person: Janie was an astronaut and it was her day off.

Second person: *Yes, but* Janie needed to buy groceries.

Third person: *Yes, but* her dog also needed walking.

First person: *Yes, but* Janie wanted to relax and read a book.

Second person: *Yes, but* Janie decided to try on a new outfit.

Third person: *Yes, but* Janie had a lot to do even though it was her day off.

Feel free to join again and be all three people. Once again, observe how you feel—take a few notes about what comes up and what you notice. Remember to always say "Yes, but" to start each sentence, after your first sentence has been created:

First person: [Insert any first sentence that comes to mind.]

Second person: *Yes, but* . . . [Add what pops up for you without thinking too much.]

Third person: *Yes, but* . . .

First person: *Yes, but* . . .

Second person: *Yes, but* . . .

Third person: *Yes, but* . . .

How did that one feel? Take a moment to consider how starting your thought with "Yes, but" influenced the conversation. What did you learn about Janie? Did this scene progress? Was there any movement forward? (We have a little back-and-forth as a larger group, for one to two minutes, on the outcomes of creating this scene when starting with the words "Yes, but," and again, we always get interesting responses from the group.)

The thing about the word "But" is it's a word that negates everything that came before you said "But." If you look at the scene above, ideas still don't move forward too well. Similar to the word "No," there's still a negative connotation. Let's face it—the words "No" and "But" stop the flow of ideas, making people feel dismissed and rejected. In an environment where "No" and "But" lead communication, people shut down and stop communicating. They check out and progress tanks. Environments feel unhealthy and tense. And like I keep saying, those words have a place—an important place—because sometimes you want to shut things down, or negate what was said before in favor of what is to come. Typically, though, you want to encourage people and demonstrate that you value and respect their input. Now, let's compare and contrast the words "No" and "But" with the words "Yes, and."

Let's try this exercise again, and this time we'll start with the words "Yes, and."

First person: Janie was an astronaut and it was her day off.

Second person: *Yes, and* Janie was excited about taking a special day trip.

Third person: *Yes, and* she brought along her dog, Max.

First person: *Yes, and* they hopped into Janie's space ship and flew to Jupiter for the day.

Second person: *Yes, and* they enjoyed a long walk discovering Jupiter's new parks.

Third person: *Yes, and* it was great that Jupiter finally had restaurants too, and a special place for dogs to play and meet other dogs.

How did "Yes, and" feel? Take a moment to consider how starting your thoughts or words with "Yes, and" changes things. What did you learn about Janie this time? Did this scene progress? Was there any movement forward? (We have a little back-and-forth as a larger group, for one to two minutes, on the outcomes of creating this scene when starting with the words "Yes, and." The group always acknowledges that when they employ "Yes, and," the scene moves forward, ideas are accepted, and there is a communication flow. There is a consensus that starting with "Yes, and" feels much more open, collaborative, positive, and supportive.

Once again, join in, and see how you feel when you start each sentence with Yes, and. Take a few notes about what comes up, and what you notice:

First person: [Insert any first sentence that comes to mind.]

Second person: *Yes, and* . . . [Add what pops up for you without thinking too much.]

Third person: *Yes, and* . . .

First person: *Yes, and* . . .

Second person: *Yes, and* . . .

Third person: *Yes, and* . . .

Inevitably, everyone feels differently about their interactions when using the words "Yes, and" to start each sentence. Words have a certain energy, and "Yes, and" evokes vitality, enthusiasm, and a sense that you're being listened to, heard, and appreciated. Definitely high-vibe. Yet beyond the positive energy something else happens as well. There's a certain flow. Movement. The scene progresses. With each sentence, a new idea emerges. With practice, "Yes, and" offers people a chance to build on each other's ideas. "Yes, and" says, "I'm listening to you. I hear you. I may agree. I may not agree. Regardless, you are being heard and respected." Starting to consider your world from a "Yes, and" perspective gets you out of conditioning, out of your thinking mind, and into a place where you're open to creativity and possibilities. "Yes, and" has potential. Growth. Progress. "Yes, and" supports people and purpose. A positive interaction between different human energies. And confident, supported, passionate human energy is what creates results. Enhances innovation and helps create a new, vibrant, and thriving company culture.

Remember that online survey I talked about in the introduction? The one where people told me what they thought about work? So many thought of it as something they had to do, drudgery, forced labor—something they did only for money.

If you put profits at the forefront of everything you do, won't your employees also put their earnings at the top? Is that the best we can do? Isn't it preferable to wake up every morning with a spring in your step, ready to face the day with gratitude, aspiration, and passion? (Okay, not every day—you know what I mean, most days).

How can we bring true, heartfelt engagement into our working lives? A psychologically healthy workplace where people feel that taking risks is encouraged. It definitely starts with listening (I did say I was going to talk about listening in every chapter). Gone are the days when senior leaders sat together in a room and hashed out the company plan, and then dumped a bunch of objectives and tasks onto employees. Right? Guess what. Wrong. This approach is still everywhere. Companies frequently change direction—demand more working hours from employees and provide few motivating reasons beyond the need for continuous company growth and profits. Look, we all know the world is in a constant state of flux. And yes, profits are important. Yet a company that puts the main focus of its efforts on revenue, at the expense of involving and championing people, is doomed to that continuous cycle of employee burnout, high rates of sick leave, and low morale. And doesn't that impact profits? As the research shows, indeed it does. This revenue-first approach is still far in the lead. The consequences are dire. What we've got is a burned-out workforce—uninspired, unmotivated, and communicating poorly. Where's the heart? The beating pulse of a great company that includes inspiring leadership, strong vision, and exciting purpose? My suggestion: when you are creating your long-term and short-term plans, include lots of continuous learning and development—for everyone. Make time to understand all team members' needs by cocreating a pathway to each individual's growth and progress. Consider a person's hopes and dreams. Involve people in the process through regular surveys, brainstorming sessions, and conversations. Create meaningful plans that are "living documents" you can change as your company changes. And listen, listen, listen. Improv can help.

Let's "Yes, And This and That"—Bringing Improv into Your Planning Cycles

Let's suppose you're a conscious leader. You've worked with other leaders and teams in your company and have created your business plan and your annual plan, and you've taken an in-depth look at the company's overall goals, business objectives, strategies, and tactics. You've reflected on how you support your desired outcomes through marketing, sales, finance, operations, customer service, and human resources. You've included all the analysis, statistics, measurable goals—everything that goes into good planning. You've gone beyond. Looked at company ethics, HR practices, how you contribute to community and the environment, the world. All the things. You're excited. You're creating a learning and development plan that supports your vision. Everyone will have lots of opportunities to learn throughout the year. Collaborate. An environment of deep trust. Does this sound like your company? Whether it does or does not, whether you have gaps in certain areas and are strong in others—regardless of where you are at: You know you need a communication strategy. For every step along the way.

Maybe your overarching vision includes creating an agile company—one where continuous change is managed effectively. Or, your focus is on adaptability—where you shift your plans quickly, based on company innovation. Perhaps your company is going through a transformation of some kind.

You need to get relational. You want to help everyone understand their roles in the process and how each person interacts with others. I've seen how the gap between creating a plan and communicating a plan is large. Often, a plan is created, it's discussed at a high level with senior executives only, and the particulars of how the plan will be executed aren't fully relayed to everyone. There's an uneasy feeling of "we think we know what we're doing," yet without the details, a fog descends that obscures true understanding.

What can we do to change that? How about adding "How we communicate" to every single section of your plan, and bringing everyone in on the "how" part? And let's make it "How we *effectively* communicate."

Improv and "Yes, And" Supports Every Aspect of Your Planning Cycle

At the broadest level, your training programs have some kind of foundation around how you:

1. Explore—determine what training is needed,
2. Design—your training programs internally and with partners,
3. Create—decide on your approach and start some initial programs, gain feedback, and
4. Apply—carry out training and evaluate effectiveness.

Through this ongoing process of deciding what training will be helpful, designing and creating programs, and then applying those programs, you're continuously deciding which types of training will be constructive. More and more innovative companies who seek experiential training tools that help leaders and teams profoundly connect are adding improv training—and regularly.

How might improv appear on your plans? You have your internal planning structure and an array of supportive approaches.

Let's suppose that your annual, quarterly, and monthly plans contain activities like planning sessions, brainstorming/ideation, leadership skills, team building, and team skills. Perhaps you've identified that part of team development includes confidence boosting and "thinking on your feet" skills to help people contribute and speak up during meetings, or improve storytelling and presentation skills.

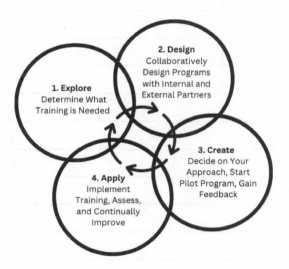

There are thousands of improv exercises, and variations on those exercises. For the sake of this example, let's look at a few of the exercises discussed in this book, in the chart that follows, and apply those exercises to your company training objectives.

COMPANY PLAN WITH IMPROV

Learning & Development Programs for Leaders and Teams

**Applied Improvisation: Non-performance improv
for skills development, Experiential Learning**

Exercises are Customized to Objectives/Planned Learning Outcomes

Improv Exercises are samples that appear throughout the book	Brainstorming/Ideation/ Creativity (Develop Vision, Mission, Values, Annual Plan)	Communication/ "Yes, And" (Skills Development, Team Building, Active Listening)
Warm up Exercises (Ice melters)		
Clap Focus	✓	✓
Red Ball	✓	✓
Greetings/Status	✓	✓
A Few Improv Standards		
Word Association	✓	✓
What Are You Doing?	✓	✓
Categories		✓
Gift-Giving		✓
Last Word Response	✓	✓
500 Year-Old-Expert		
No, But, Yes, And	✓	✓
Rants		
Dr. Know It All		✓
Thank You Statues	✓	✓
Thank You Conversation	✓	✓

The power of debriefs: As you can see, the exercise examples can be modified to suit many different objectives. The magic is in the debriefs, the explanations that take place at the end of each exercise, grounding the experience in language that supports your goals and desired outcomes.

Leadership Skills (Self-Awareness, Storytelling, Confidence)	Sales Skills, Public Speaking, Collaboration ("Thinking on Your Feet," Vulnerability, Presence)
✓	✓
✓	✓
✓	✓
✓	✓
✓	✓
✓	✓
	✓
	✓
	✓
✓	✓
✓	✓
✓	✓
	✓
✓	✓

The Importance of Debriefs

Many improv exercises can be applied to a variety of situations. For example, Gift-Giving can help build connection, empathy, the give and take of "Yes, and," active listening, and more. After each exercise, the facilitator leads a brief conversation about the value of the exercise to the particular circumstance, or objective. If a team is working on building connection and trust, for example, the facilitator will focus in on this topic during the debrief. The beauty of debriefs is when people are invited to chime in with their reflections and insights, making the experience personal and powerfully conscious.

Leading Your Team with Gratitude

As we move toward the end of our journey together, it strikes me that leading with gratitude is always a great way to communicate. It's a great way to start our day, with our own internal practice, and it's great for teams. I'd like to present one final exercise which is called "Thank You Conversations," which is always well received and supports team bonding.

For this exercise, participants are standing around the room in pairs as I walk around listening to their conversations. All they have to do is have a conversation about anything that arises, and before each sentence, they say "thank you" to each other.

> First person: Thank you, John, how are you doing today?

> Second person: Thank you, Sally, I'm doing well, you?

First person: Thank you, John, I'm feeling pretty well, although I had a little trouble getting here today.

Second person: Thank you, Sally, really. I'm sorry to hear that. What happened?

First person: Thank you, John. My alarm didn't go off and I'm adjusting to this time zone. There's a six-hour difference.

Second person: Thank you, Sally. Wow. I can imagine that would be tough. I'm feeling for you.

I continue walking around the room and I hear:

First person: Thank you, Jim, it's great to meet you.

Second person: Thank you, Tina, wonderful to meet you too.

First person: Thank you, Jim, I wanted to let you know about a project that is having a challenge.

Second person: Thank you, Tina, is it that special assignment one?

First person: Thank you, Jim. Yes. The deliverables are all late, and I'm at a loss as to how to proceed.

Second person: Thank you, Tina. Geez. Yes. Let's work together on this. We are where we are, and we can plan for where we're at.

As you can see, expressing gratitude before each sentence totally removes any tension from each situation. Instead, the words "thank you" elicit a kind of empathy—we're in it together and we've got each other's back. After I lead this exercise, everyone typically leaves the room saying "thank you," and later, as I pass them in the hall, they start their sentences with me by saying, "thank you." "Thank you, Tracy, that was super fun and I also learned a lot." What a wonderful tribute to the experience of gratitude, and how this exercise had quickly changed their states, opening them to a feeling of grace.

Try it yourself. See how you feel when you start your sentence with "thank you." And for fun, you can be both people if you are alone, or maybe recruit a family member for this one (good for the family too).

> First person: Thank you . . ."
>
> Second person: Thank you . . ."
>
> First person: Thank you . . ."
>
> Second person: Thank you . . ."

And so on—no need to stop at four lines, of course. Let the conversation start and stop naturally. And take a moment at the end to reflect on how you felt and what you noticed. How did it feel to say "thank you" to one another? What did you notice about the conversation—did you experience a broader quality of gratitude? There's a compounding impact to gratitude when we express it throughout our day. This exercise links to the "I'm grateful" team mentioned in the "Flash Forward" section in chapter 2, and also the affirmations in chapter 5. If you can add gratitude to your individual, team, and company practices, you will notice a positive shift in how everything flows, and how people cooperate.

"Yes, And–ing" Business Today and Into the Future

The interesting part of all this "Yes, and–ing" is that improv doesn't just stop after you've done the exercise. You've had a positive effect on one another that you will remember—and the brain remembers too. It's all about training the brain. The team that plays together, stays together . . . and also experiences gratitude and connection, builds trust, and, as research shows, increases their levels of good brain hormones like dopamine, serotonin, and oxytocin, while decreasing stress hormones like cortisol.

Yet of course, it's not just the chemicals. When your team shows up with gratitude for one another, it's pretty hard to bring a condescending or contemptuous attitude to a situation. The words "thank you" offer an emotional bond that lets teammates know you're in it together.

The business world is always changing at lightning speed, and companies seeking to stay competitive must be both agile and resilient. Adaptable. Learning and development are important tools to help leaders and teams access those strengths. When you invite people to get curious, explore leading-edge training techniques, and equip people with new skills, they adapt to change more efficiently. If tough situations arise, people respond more flexibly. Rigidity melts away and relationships improve—not only within teams, also from leaders and teams to cross-functional, stakeholders, and customers. Yes, it is vital in these times that companies offer training in the open flow of expression—sharing thoughts and feelings with vulnerability.

Because nothing happens well without effective communication. Strong communication equates to the flow of creativity too.

Across the globe, companies—and their vast array of visions and cultures—are rising and falling. What makes some succeed while others fail? There can be no doubt that effective communication skills are critical. Strong communication, with a "Yes, and" attitude, leads to creativity and innovation too. As we've established in these pages, it's the human element that keeps a business vibrant. Those companies that slow down to listen to their people, that celebrate the voices and ideas of their teams, surge forward with the energy of their employees. Communication training is unparalleled at bringing about these results.

As a conscious improvisational leader, a key part of your job is to provide consistent opportunities and instruction that supports people, so they know their ideas are valued. You want to instill a sense of purpose and encourage a team dynamic of engagement. As you envision your next steps, you may want to generate something absolutely new. Or, you may choose to build atop what remains of previous plans. Leading with heart is imperative, since people rise up and meet the moment based on how they feel, not because of what they think. That's why effective leadership is an inside job first—other people respond to what you feel too. You want to make that inner work a regular practice. Improv gets into your body, disrupts the judge in your brain, and brings you to a place of openness. This open space, beyond ego and conditioning, is where true change happens—for you, your team, your organization, and indeed the world. Thank you, Dear Leader. Together, let's create a "Yes, and" world.

Chapter Summary

- In a "Yes, and" company culture, leaders and teams cocreate clear goals, values, and attitudes that are agreed upon and communicated.

- Creating a "Yes, and" culture means a focus on people and purpose, that supports employee engagement and retention.

- Communicating with "Yes, and," when compared to communicating with "No" or "Yes, But," demonstrates the value of leading with a "Yes, and" perspective.

- Bringing improv into your company creates a culture of storytelling, ideation, and positive team bonding.

- Leading with gratitude and heart shows you care about people and builds trust.

- The playfulness of improv invites laughter, the great universal language that will keep your team connected.

- Start saying, "Let's 'Yes, and' this and that," and experience how the flow of "giving and receiving" ideas transforms your leadership and your life.

ABOUT THE AUTHOR

Tracy Shea-Porter

Tracy Shea-Porter is the CEO and cofounder of Yes Unlimited, with an extensive background in Applied Improvisation and corporate communications, marketing, and sales. Her improvisation background combines with her business experience to inspire and motivate leaders and teams to flourish by bringing improv skills and "Yes, and" communication to their work. She holds a BA degree with distinction from the University of Toronto and is a member of ACTRA (Alliance of Canadian Cinema, Television and Radio Artists) and a Professional Member of AIN (Applied Improvisation Network).

When Tracy ventured down to Theatresports and discovered improvisation at Toronto's Harbourfront in 1987, she could not have guessed that she would become part of the improv scene, spanning some thirty-five years and counting. As she explored improv, she also held various positions in communications management and corporate sales. Yes Unlimited was born through her collaboration with Yes Unlimited cofounder and renowned improv teacher Ralph MacLeod, owner of the SoCap theatre in Toronto. Tracy, Ralph, and the Yes Unlimited team of improviser facilitators have designed and delivered improv training and event experiences to a diverse range of international clients, including Accenture, CAMH, CIHI, Constellation Software/Perseus Group, Foglers, Humber College, Metrolinx,

Ship Apollo, The Source, the University of Toronto, and the Whitby Chamber of Commerce, among many others. Yes Unlimited enjoys a valued partnership with Great Place to Work Canada, an international organization that certifies companies as great workplaces through confidential employee surveys that uncover actionable insights. Tracy is a lover of live music, art, nature, film, bicycle riding, and, of course, improv. She is a mentor for the University of Toronto's Backpack to Briefcase and Next Steps programs. Tracy lives in Toronto and is deeply grateful for her daily video chats and in-person gatherings with her daughter Allysha and Flo the Cat.

Improv Exercises
and Practices at a Glance

In improv, the exercises are the teachers. And yes, it would be a definite benefit to bring in an experienced improviser, facilitator, or trainer (frequently Applied Improvisation facilitators are all three) who can work with and guide you and your team, as you invite improv into your team training world. An objective eye adds that external clarity to your learning and development programs. As well, those working with improv training on a regular basis are practiced, adaptable, and frequently well-versed at bringing forth a dynamic quality that engages participants. They also have the ability to debrief "on the fly" about the value of improv to your particular focus and learning objectives.

Those who teach improv often have a keen sense around individual and group behaviors and can hone in on areas of focus to help people grow. And, in the spirit of "Yes, and," a "train the trainers" program is another way to bring improv into your company. If you have an internal training team, why not have them work with experienced improv facilitators to learn improv techniques? You can even enlist a back-and-forth approach—combining an internal and external training experience as you go. There is definitely something unique and marvelous about working with trained and experienced facilitators who have that remarkable flavor combination of teaching improv, facilitation skills, and a background in performance. After all, improv is experiential, and when you work with trained improviser facilitators, you get the full improv experience.

In the main section of this book, I focused on just a few exercises to illustrate case studies through real-world examples. The goal was to show some of the proven ways that improv is an important training tool for you and your company. There are thousands of exercises and just as many case studies. There are improv approaches to facilitate everything from creating your plans and brainstorming to establishing values for your company to developing storytelling and presentation skills. And, of course, that highly requested training—team building and bonding.

The length of time for an improv training can vary depending on group experience, group size, and what flows in the moment. For groups under twenty-five, improv typically happens with everyone on their feet and standing in a circle. This type of session is often ninety minutes to two hours, although it can go longer too. On the other hand, if you have a hundred people, you might have four breakout rooms of twenty to twenty-five people per room to ensure a meaningful experience, where everyone is participating. And you can also hold large group events, which means people are seated and the exercises are demonstrated at the front of the room (in this scenario, your team members are invited to participate as audience volunteers). These are a few of the ways Applied Improvisers conduct improv training. Of course, there are many more approaches, including full-day or multiday events, the inclusion of role-playing, and making improv a part of a larger, themed company experience such as planning sessions, training days, or sales rallies, to name a few.

To add to your sense of how improv works, and the benefits "Yes, and" provides, the appendix contains an at-a-glance view of the exercises presented through this book. As discussed at the start of this book, these exercises are not presented in a "train the trainers" format. Rather, they are taste tests for you to review. The idea is for you to see how improv training connects beautifully to your learning and development programs. To plan your improv training, you will want to have a conversation with an improviser facilitator, who can learn more about your objectives and talk about different approaches and options.

Icemelters and Warm-up Exercises

At the start of each improv training event, we provide a quick breakdown of what improv is and who we are, as well as a demonstration of what to expect. In doing so, we highlight the need to suspend judgment (particularly of ourselves) and embrace courage building, as well as the group support that exists when we step out of our boxes and take a risk.

Short improv icemelters help people bond, focus, and get grounded and ready to collaborate.

All exercises are facilitator led, and there is a lively conversation between the improv trainer and the participants throughout the workshop. Debriefs after each exercise, which relay the important takeaways of the exercise, help people connect each exercise to its intended purpose. Further grounding of the exercise to match its objective occurs as participants engage in the debrief and bring in their views and experiences. Of course, laughter is guaranteed—that great, universal language that breaks through ego, alleviates stress, and boosts morale.

These excellent icemelters serve as warm-up exercises to help participants get into the improv state of mind and start to build a team flow. The facilitator naturally moves from one exercise to the next as the group focus shifts, as people become adept at each exercise, and as learning goals are achieved.

Clap Focus

Clap focus is a standard improv exercise that is often employed to start an event, inviting people to listen, respond, and react without thinking. Everyone is in a circle. One person is directed to make eye contact with another member of the group and clap toward them. The person who accepts the clap focus then makes eye contact with another person and claps toward them. As the group gets comfortable giving and receiving the clap focus, the exercise speeds up and synergy is created among participants.

Debrief focuses on the importance of eye contact, direct communication, keeping your head up, and being engaged in your environment. Conversation points include how to give and receive messages during complex times, when thousands of messages are received daily.

Red Ball

The red ball exercise may follow clap focus if the facilitator wants to continue to ground the group in the improv experience. Standing in a circle, the group throws an imaginary red ball back and forth, in a similar way to clap focus. As people gain confidence, the instructor adds more balls with varying colors. As the exercise progresses, there may be several different colored balls moving at once, requiring everyone to stay fully present and engaged.

Debrief focuses on ways to ensure a message is received and the challenges and myths of multitasking. Conversation points include importance of making sure your message is received, and how "the ball may get dropped" when too many distractions are taking place and it's difficult to focus.

Greetings/Status

The facilitator leads the members of the group to move around the room saying hello to each other. When prompted by the facilitator, the intention of the greeting will change. Intentions can include: greet each other like you would greet a close friend, someone you don't like, a rival, a person you don't trust. The facilitator will decide on the length of time for each interaction (usually 10 to 20 seconds), and will provide the intention.

Debrief focuses on verbal and nonverbal cues of communication and the ways they impact the receiver. Great introduction to status, including ways we give and receive status, and the power and relationship dynamics between people. Conversation points include how we show up in different situations and how we respond to other people based on preconceived perceptions.

A Few Improv Standards (10–25 minutes each)

Improv exercises are selected to suit the objectives of a workshop or training. Exercises can often be modified to adapt to a particular goal. It's really all about the debrief—the conversation that facilitator and attendees engage in to "unpack" the learnings of each improv exercise.

Word Association

Still in the circle, or in a line, the facilitator starts with one word. Based on that word, the next person in line says the first word that pops up for them, and so on. (For example, if Person A says "crayon," Person B might say "draw," and then Person C might say "cloud," and so on). During this word game, there are typically judgements that arise. For example, a person may shrug their shoulders when they say a word, as though their word is not a good choice. Or a person will turn the word into a question, through an upward intonation, indicating they are not confident. The exercise teaches acceptance of a choice, including your own, and how to collaborate and build momentum as a team.

Debrief focuses on letting go of judgment of ideas, and the importance of verbal and nonverbal cues to demonstrate acceptance and confidence. Conversation points include how opening up to creativity and accepting all ideas builds trust and team cooperation.

What Are You Doing?

The whole group is in a circle, and the facilitator invites one person (Person A) into the middle. This person will start doing an activity suggested by the facilitator (e.g., skiing). The facilitator will ask a second person (Person B) to enter the circle and ask "What are you doing?" The person who is skiing will continue skiing, yet they will name a different activity, such as reading a book. Person B will then start reading a book (and Person A will leave the circle). Next, the facilitator will invite Person C to enter the circle and ask Person B "What are you doing?" Person B, who is reading a book, will name another activity, such as climbing a mountain. Person C will start climbing a mountain (and Person B will leave the circle). This exercise will continue until everyone has had one to two turns.

Debrief focuses on how offering your teammate an activity helps them succeed and builds trust. Also, accepting your teammate's idea as a gift, sets everyone up for success. When you open to the power of the group dynamic, positive cooperation grows. Conversation points include importance of accepting ideas as a pathway to team bonding. This exercise also supports your ability to multitask in a fun way, as you stretch your brain to say one thing while doing another.

Categories

Participants are moved into a line of six to ten people. Facilitator asks for a category, such as types of flowers. Facilitator then points to a person at random and they name a type of flower, such as a rose. Facilitator continues to point at people in the line randomly until someone cannot come up with a type of flower, and that person exits the game. (No repeats are allowed—once the first person says *rose*, *rose* is off the table.) After the first person is eliminated, a new category is selected, such as cities. The facilitator points at people who then state a city name, until someone cannot come up with a city. That person exits. The game continues until one person is left. The facilitator then selects a final category, such as movie titles. The final person then says movie titles until they can't think of any more. Everyone has a chance to experience failure and learns to identify losing with learning and growth—while having fun.

Debrief revolves around the idea that we're all part of the same journey, operating as a cohesive team where mutual support is paramount. This activity fosters camaraderie and shared laughter, even as we collectively navigate moments of setback and failure, viewing them as valuable learning experiences. Conversation points include the idea that every individual encounters challenges, and it's through our support for one another that we cultivate team growth. When someone faces a setback in one of the categories, the entire group rallies behind them, providing an opportunity for the individual to exemplify 'grace under pressure.'

Gift-Giving

Facilitator invites people to form groups of two, and offers participants a question to ask one another, such as "What lights you up?" or "What's your favorite hobby or memory?" Person A asks the question—for example, "What lights you up?" Person B, as an example, answers, "I love the artist Vincent van Gogh." Person A then says, "May I present you with this special van Gogh blanket featuring his painting *The Starry Night*. The partners then switch, so each person gives and receives an imaginary gift. This gift exchange can go back and forth a few times.

Debrief focuses on how gift giving invites a vulnerability, as you reveal some of your favorite memories or things to do. This activity invites trust building, empathy, and connection. People may be encouraged to work with someone they don't know as well, to continue building rapport and camaraderie between team members. Conversation points include how gratitude supports team bonding, and how kind-hearted exchanges help people build faith in one another.

Last Word Response

Everyone is in a circle, and facilitator invites participants to break into pairs. In each pair, Person A starts a conversation by saying a sentence—it can be about whatever they like. Then, Person B has to reply, starting their reply with the last word of Person A's sentence. The two participants go back and forth for the length of the exercise, always starting with the last word of their partner's sentence. For example, if Person A says, "It is a beautiful day for hiking" then Person B stars their sentence with the word "hiking," such as, "Hiking is one of my favorite activities for fitness."

Debrief focuses on the instinct to interrupt and how much information we miss when we "listen to respond," as opposed to "listen to understand." Conversation points include the importance of active listening in all our communications, and how we easily miss information when we "tune out" what other people are relaying. Listening to a person all the way to the end of the last word they speak shows respect and builds connection.

500-Year-Old Expert

The facilitator invites participants to form groups of four. In their groups, team members describe a fictional product in four stages: to a 1500s audience, 1950s audience, present day audience, and future audience. The fictional product may be provided by the facilitator, so all groups are focusing on one product, such as a flying machine. Person A pitches the product to the other three team members using made-up language in the style of the 1500s. The other three team members are the customers, who can ask questions and seek more information. Then, Person B will pitch the product to the three team members in a 1950s style, and so on. This exercise can be repeated until everyone has had a turn presenting their product for different time periods.

Debrief focuses on the need to understand your audience's frame of reference, use their language, and stay open to new approaches. Great for sales teams, brainstorming, and ideation. Conversation points include how to relay information in an impromptu way and pivoting to the needs of your customer or stakeholder.

"No," "Yes, But," and "Yes, And"

For this exercise, the facilitator invites the group to form trios. The facilitator asks each group to tell a simple fictional story, and may provide the first line, such as "Nancy took a walk with her dog, Pal." The group then tells the story, and each line starts with the word "No."

> Person A: Nancy took a walk with her dog, Pal.
>
> Person B: No, she went to the store.
>
> Person C: No, actually, Nancy went to the airport to fly to Europe.

(The story can continue for about a minute with everyone using the word "No" to start their sentence).

Quick debrief occurs to see how everyone is feeling about using the word "No." Typically, people see that "No" shuts down conversation and stops the flow of ideas, so there is no forward movement.

The exercise continues, using the same story, and this time everyone starts their sentences with the word "Yes, but."

> Person A: Nancy took a walk with her dog, Pal.

> Person B: Yes, but she forgot that she really needed to call her friend.

> Person C: Yes, but she noticed her dog actually needed to have lunch.

(The story can continue for about a minute with everyone using the words "Yes, but" to start their sentence).

Quick debrief occurs to see how everyone is feeling about using the word "But." Typically, people notice that "But" also slows or halts conversation. The word "But" also appears to be somewhat negative, and negates whatever is said before the use of the word "But," shutting down ideas.

The exercise continues, using the same story, and this time everyone starts their sentences with the phrase "Yes, and."

> Person A: Nancy took a walk with her dog, Pal.

> Person B: Yes, and on the way, she met up with a neighbour and her dog, Ruff, and they went to the dog park together.

Person C: Yes, and while at the dog park, Pal and Ruff met a whole group of their friends.

(The story can continue for about a minute with everyone using the phrase "Yes, and" to start their sentence.)

Debrief focuses on effective language choices, how to use "Yes, and" to turn difficult conversations into collaborative ones, and how to stay open in any situation. Conversation points include why "Yes, and" nurtures collaborative teamwork and creates opportunities to brainstorm, as well as how, as the foundational principle of improv, "Yes, and" supports overall effective communication skills.

Rants

In a circle or a line, the facilitator provides four to eight people with an attitude and a topic, such as "loving pizza with pineapple" or "suspicious of shoelaces." Facilitator tells each person to "rant" about their topic by pointing at an individual or saying their name. In this way, the facilitator directs the participants to "rant" on cue. Eventually, participants operate like a symphony, as the facilitator leads them back and forth quickly.

Debrief focuses on "thinking on your feet," storytelling, confidence, and overcoming fear of failure. Conversation points include impromptu conversations and how exercising your "impromptu" muscle helps you get in the flow of speaking up in the moment.

Ad Game

Facilitator invites team to form groups of three to eight people. The game starts with the suggestion of a fictional product (a car, a shoe, a lamp). The facilitator will direct the group to reveal the details about this exciting new product they've created. To start, Person A will be guided to make a statement about the product, such as "This car has flying machine capabilities." Everyone will support this idea with a zealous "Yes!" Person B will contribute another idea, such as "And the flying wings on the car take instructions and self-drive to your destination." Everyone supports all ideas with a positive "Yes!" This process continues for a few minutes until the product feels complete. Then, the product also receives a name from the group, a tagline, and a celebrity who endorses the product. Finally, the group will talk together for a few moments, and then they can present a twenty- to thirty-second improvised commercial about their new creation.

Debrief focuses on how listening and agreement support team spirit and growth. When applying the "Yes, and" principle to creating a product, all ideas are heard, accepted, and acknowledged. Conversation points include ways that cooperation between team members—and different departments—contributes to a greater outcome, where collaboration improves the product or brand.

Thank You Conversations

The facilitator invites the group to form pairs, and invites participants to engage in a conversation in which, each time they speak, they begin with the words "Thank you" and the other person's name. The conversations can be about anything, and the point is to offer acknowledgement. For example, Person A might say, "Thank you, Janet, I just arrived at this conference, and I'm excited to learn more about the team." Person B might say, "Thank you, John, I just arrived here as well, and the team is here from all over the world." The conversation can continue in different directions, and the point is to continue to recognize the other person.

Debrief focuses on the effect that "Thank you" has and how this powerful phrase can be used to deflate an emotionally charged conversation, and how the simple two words of "Thank you" create a spirit of team gratitude and camaraderie. Conversation may include how acknowledgement helps your teammates feel heard, understood, and valued, and can contribute to team bonding.

A Note About Improv Exercises and the History of Applied Improvisation: It's important to acknowledge that all of the exercises discussed in this book are improv standards—foundational, well-established improv exercises—that have been created, tweaked, changed, and adapted to all manner of applications over the past several decades. The exercises have been handed down through teachings, from one improviser to the next, through thousands upon thousands of hours of improv training, classes, and events, as well as through stagecraft. An attempt to give credit to the creator of a particular exercise is therefore a challenge. However, it's definitely important to attribute the creation of improv methods to both Viola Spolin—considered the mother of improvisational theater and the author of *Improvisation for the Theater*—and Keith Johnstone, another improv legend, and the author of the classic *Impro: Improvisation and the Theatre*. Furthermore, the roots of Applied Improvisation (that nonperformance approach to improv we are discussing here) started in the late 1990s, and the Applied Improvisation Network (AIN) was founded in 2002 by Paul Z. Jackson, Michael Rosenburg, and Alain Rostain. Building on these roots, improvisers around the world contribute their unique voices and visions to improv on a daily basis. And, as is the nature of improv, they continue to try out the exercises, make mistakes, adapt, try again, fail as hard as they can, and grow. It's playtime!

GLOSSARY OF TERMS

Creativity is not the clever rearranging of the known.

—Viola Spolin

Throughout this book, I've employed some terms particular to Applied Improvisation and other areas that support the improv techniques we are exploring through this book. Some of these words or phrases may be familiar, and some may be new—or your definition and interpretation of them may be a little different from my intended purpose. So, in this glossary, I've provided brief and simple definitions for a number of terms that apply to our work together. Go ahead and take a look.

Acceptance—When you practice acceptance, you agree to the reality of a situation. In improv, acceptance means you are above all listening to another person, and at the same time accepting their offer or choice. You make your teammate "look good" by accepting their idea, and you build on their idea with your own idea.

Acknowledgment—Acknowledgment is the act of, well, acknowledging something or someone. Through improv, you learn to listen to people effectively and acknowledge what they say and their opinions. The point of acknowledgment in improv is that you are hearing another person and respecting their ideas.

Active Listening—When you are actively listening, you actually prepare to listen, and listen with intention. You move beyond simply hearing the words spoken, and you seek to understand. In improv, we often talk about being fully present, rather than preparing your own response while you listen. In other words, you try to stop thinking about your response, and focus solely on being present and tuning in. Active listening builds trust and helps you understand other perspectives. You pay conscious attention to another person's verbal and nonverbal messages, so that person feels seen, heard, and validated. Active listening supports empathy and perspective taking skills.

Adaptability—In business, adaptability means you can adjust to new conditions and can challenge yourself to change as your circumstances change. Improv helps you hone your adaptability skills by teaching you how to be more flexible, open, and willing to embrace new ideas and conversation shifts.

Affirmations—Affirmations are positive statements you can create, or find through research, to reaffirm personal values and focus on positive outcomes. Affirmations help you come from a place of gratitude.

Agility—To be agile is to be quick and alert. Through improv, you learn to pay attention—in the moment, through active listening and awareness skills, all of which helps you be more agile.

Alter Ego—An alter ego is another version of yourself, like a "character" or "persona" you create for certain situations. For example, people may employ an alter ego to gain more confidence when presenting or onstage. As you create a character in a scene, such as through improv, that character can become an alter ego. A role can take on a life of its own, separate from who you are in real life.

Applied Improvisation—Applied Improvisation refers to a training and coaching approach that takes theories, practices, and exercises from improv theater and adapts them to develop behaviors and skills for other professional environments. Examples of those skills include effective leadership, team communication, and creativity expansion.

Authentic Self—Your authentic self is who you are at your deepest core. When what you say in life aligns with your actions. Improv also invites you to express your authentic self by taking risks and opening up to collaborate effectively with your teammates.

Awareness—At the basic level, when you are aware, you understand, perceive, and are conscious of events. As it relates to improv, awareness is also about being in touch with what another person is saying, doing, and feeling. Awareness combines listening and seeing another person, so you feel a sense of connection. You are present and aware of another, giving your full attention to the situation at hand. Therefore, you are not caught up in your thoughts or thinking about something else. Your attention is on what is happening in the moment.

Balance—Balance may be defined as an equilibrium, or a state in which conflicting or opposite forces or influences find a balance (like yin and yang). You may seek a balanced life through a balance of habits and practices that support your work and life. The planet requires balance to thrive, as another example. Through the practice of improv, you can balance your ideas with the ideas of other people, learning to cocreate and collaborate. Improv helps you see the world around you in new ways, inviting a "give and receive" openness that supports balanced viewpoints.

Believe—When you truly believe something, it becomes truth to you. In improv, fully engaging in an exercise with your authentic self lets you discover the moment through engagement and belief in what you are doing and experiencing. The power of believing is a well-known confidence booster that helps you overcome self-doubt and take action on your ideas.

Best Practice—A best practice is a method or technique that has been assessed as having produced positive results, generally over time. When you are in the process of creating something in business, such as a set of values or a learning and development program, you may research best practices to help you make decisions and choices.

Bold Candor—At work, the phrase "bold candor" has come to signify open and honest expression. Sometimes, being bold means that you are making suggestions that are outside the current norms. Improv supports bold candor by encouraging you to voice yourself in imaginary ways first, helping you to get in touch with your own authentic voice.

Brainstorming—When you are brainstorming, you are problem-solving and inviting spontaneity into a collaboration with other people. Everyone is invited to say whatever arises, to offer as many ideas as possible. During brainstorming, an idea might spark another idea, and so everyone can feel free to add whatever they are thinking. I like to say that during brainstorming, "all ideas are good ideas." Improv is excellent for brainstorming, as the group can lead with "Yes, and" and apply exercises that help people open up to collaborate. When you're "Yes, and–ing" during brainstorming sessions, you can leave the critical thinking for another day.

Breathwork—Through various breathing practices, you can positively impact your mental, emotional, and physical states. Attention to breathwork before a stressful event, such as presenting, can help you become calmer. Being aware of your breath when practicing improv helps you get in touch with how effective breathing supports all areas of your life.

But—The word "But" presents a contrast between two or more items. For example, one might say, "She went to work, but she forgot her lunch." The word "But" negates or cancels out everything that goes before it, and so when using the word "But," you want to ensure that this way of communicating matches your intention.

Collaboration—A collaboration means two or more people are working together to finish a task or accomplish a goal. Improv supports effective collaboration through exercises that teach active listening, how to stay open and receptive to new ideas while also sharing your own, and how to stay present while engaging with enthusiasm in the moment.

Collective Consciousness—A collective consciousness arises within groups as they embrace a set of shared beliefs, ideas, and visions together. Every team and company has its own unique collective consciousness that changes as people change and company missions evolve. Improv helps leaders and teams effectively communicate by helping them share ideas, speak up, and get creative, leading to a more in-tune collective consciousness.

Comfort Zones—A comfort zone is the place where you function with ease and familiarity. Stretching your comfort zone is important because it leads to personal growth. Improv is a great way to stretch your comfort zone because it offers a "low-stakes" way to try new things, leading to personal expansion.

185

Common Ground—Finding common ground is a way for people to agree about something even if they do not agree about everything. Common ground requires communication, and that leads to trust. The practice of improv helps people achieve common ground as they learn how to listen to ideas, accept them (even if they don't agree), and engage in back-and-forth communication until they find common ground.

Communication—Communication is all about how we show up in the world, including how we communicate with ourselves and other people. How we speak, move, listen, and interpret—all of the verbal and nonverbal cues that reveal something about us and how we relate to the world. Communication is associated with every term on this list, as communication is the broad, overarching subject of this book. What is effective communication and how are people communicating around the world every day? What are the barriers to effective communication? What can we do to help? We all need to communicate many times throughout each day, and it helps to observe ourselves and become aware of our role in communication. How do you communicate, and what are your communication practices?

Conditioned Mind—Everyone has a conditioned mind, which is based on what we learn in our formative years and beyond, as well as how we interpret the world through our particular lens. Improv invites you to challenge what you think, as well as your "collection of stories," which have accumulated based on every experience you've ever had. Improv helps you stay open and curious, exploring imagination and new ways of viewing the world.

Conditioning—Conditioning is associated with ego and constructs. We are all conditioned, and we want to continuously observe our conditioning through awareness practices. Conditioning is a set of beliefs we adhere to as a result of everything we've ever learned, including where we are born, what family we grew up in, and everything that's happened to us to create our egos. Conditioning helps us move about in the world and yet also limits our view of the world.

Confidence—When you feel confident, you have a feeling of self-assurance and present yourself with ease in your own abilities. Improv helps you improve your confidence, as you let go of perfectionism and embrace making mistakes as a pathway to growth. You learn to cocreate and understand it's not on you to have all the answers. As you deeply listen to other people and also feel the value of being truly heard, you learn that confidence is about simply being your authentic self, learning, and growing.

Connection—When you feel seen and valued by another person, you feel a connection. Through improv, authentic human connections are formed when people exchange ideas with positive energy and listen to understand, rather than to simply reply. True connection builds trust.

Convergent Thinking—Convergent thinking is a term coined by Joy Paul Guilford to describe the process of choosing the most logical answer to a problem. Convergent thinking is the opposite of divergent thinking. It generally involves giving the "correct" answer to problems or situations that do not require significant creativity.

Cooperation—When people cooperate, they are working together to achieve the same goal. Improv supports cooperation, as you engage in exercises spontaneously, leading you to give and receive through acceptance, listening, and building on each other's ideas, while deferring judgment.

Conscious Leader—A conscious leader practices self-awareness and cultivates progress in companies by encouraging and supporting individual and team growth. This type of leader has a "we" approach rather than a "me" approach, and is collaborative and open to other ideas. Improv, as a team skill, supports conscious leaders as they develop and help their teams evolve and contribute.

Constructs—Constructs make the world go around. They are the common language and shared set of meanings that help us to communicate. We need constructs. We also have to be aware that constructs may restrain us, limiting us to a certain view of the world and causing us to prejudge situations. Like the ego, constructs have a necessary place in the world—and also must be continually reconsidered through a constant practice of awareness and observation.

Courage—Courage can be defined as having the ability to persevere even though something seems difficult or creates fear. Improv supports courage and courage building as you jump in, try new things on the spot, and stretch your comfort zone.

Creativity—When you are creative, you make use of your imagination to access original ideas. When you practice improv, you also activate your imagination, opening to new ways of viewing situations and leading to innovation.

Curiosity—Curiosity is an eagerness around learning and growing. Through improv, you invite curiosity, suspend judgment, and unblock rigid thinking in order to accept ideas.

Debriefs—A debrief is an intentional conversation meant to help solidify your knowledge or a skill. In improv, after exercises, the facilitator may hold a debrief about the meaning of the exercise as it relates to your goal or objective. Furthermore, the input from participants during improv can expand the debrief and help tap into a shared meaning through group interaction.

Disruption—In this context, disruption is about disrupting old patterns and ways of seeing the world. Improv helps you disrupt the judge in your brain as you access new ideas, creativity, and imagination.

Divergent Thinking—Divergent thinking is a thought process or method to generate creative ideas by exploring many possible solutions. Improv is known to support divergent thinking. It typically occurs in a spontaneous, free-flowing, "non-linear" manner.

Ego—Your collection of thoughts. Your box of stories. Each ego is unique, individual, and based on every single experience you've ever had—becoming thought-forms in the mind. When we have any experience, we judge it based on what our past history tells us. The ego has a strong and valuable purpose, as it informs us as we go about the world. The ego also constantly runs amok, telling us false stories—running continuous thought streams—and trying to keep us safe using the fight-or-flight response. The ego is both our friend and our adversary. We need to keep an eye on the ego through awareness and observation practices.

Empathy—Empathy can be defined as the ability to understand and share the feelings of another person. Through improv, you tap into your empathy as you truly listen, hear, and seek to understand other points of view.

Energy—Human Power—or every body system that comprises a human—results in energy being produced. We share our energy person by person as we interact on a daily basis. When engaging in improv scenes, we share energy back and forth with other people through play and laughter.

Experiential, or Experiential Learning—When you engage in experiential learning, you learn by doing. Improv is highly experiential, as you take part in exercises that encourage you to be "thinking on your feet," responding spontaneously in the moment, and making things up on the spot.

Fear, or Fear of Failure—When we are afraid, we feel stressed and threatened. Fear is an important feeling that helps us recognize danger. In today's world, we may also experience fear when we are trying new things, which often keeps us in our comfort zones. Improv invites us to overcome fear of failure through laughter, as we step out of our comfort zones and learn that failure is an important part of any growth.

Give and Receive—Improv is all about giving and receiving ideas through "Yes, and" principles. The idea is to apply active listening skills while another is speaking, and to build on another person's idea with your idea (without planning your response while the other person is talking). This flow of giving and receiving results in a positive interaction where you stay open to ideas, let go of the need to control, and find new common ground.

Gratitude—When we feel gratitude, we focus on what's good in our lives and being thankful. In improv, as we listen to and accept offers from our partners, we feel a sense of gratitude because we feel connection. Feeling grateful corresponds to improvement in handling stress, cultivating happiness, and team bonding.

Habits—A habit can be defined as a routine that we practice regularly. Most people are a mix of good and bad habits, which together shape the quality of our lives. An improvisational mindset can help you break out of daily routines and unlock new ideas, both personally and professionally. This openness to change can result in improved life and workplace habit forming.

Heart-Led Leadership—When you are a heart-led leader, you have compassion and empathy for other people. Being a heart-led leader does not mean a person is "soft" in an inefficient way; rather, it means you are authentic, self-aware, and acting from integrity.

High-Vibe—High-vibe is a positive, feel-good place to be. When you practice gratitude and focus on breathwork and mindfulness, you tend to feel that high energetic frequency.

Humor—When you find a topic or event funny, you employ your sense of humor. Through improv, you engage in shared humor through playfulness, which helps people bond.

Icemelters—An icemelter is a warm-up exercise that helps get people grounded, present, and focused. In improv, it's an activity that helps "melt the ice" between people, letting them prepare for the main exercises about to happen.

Ideation—In brief, ideation is the formation of ideas or concepts. In a business context, ideation is a creative process for generating new ideas. Improv can help leaders and teams brainstorm effectively, open up to working together on solving challenges, and come up with innovative ideas and solutions.

Imagination—Imagination is the ability of a mind to be creative or resourceful. Improv encourages people to stretch their imaginations, as people open to new scenarios and ideas on the spot, without planning or scripts.

Impromptu—Impromptu is an event that is not planned, rehearsed, or organized. Improv is an impromptu activity since everything is made up in the moment, creating a free-form experience.

Improv—Improv, which is the short from of the word improvisation, is a theatrical technique. As spontaneous ensemble theater, improv is an art form through which performers make up scenes on the spot.

Improviser—An improviser is a person who invents or creates something without any prior planning. One may improvise in an improv scene with other members of a theatrical group, or an improviser might present a speech on the spot, without a script or advance preparation.

Improvisation—Improvisation, the long form of "improv," is the action of improvising. Whether it's a free-form style of jazz or a set of actors performing without a script, improvisation is the act of coming up with something in the moment.

Improvisational Leader—An improvisational leader is able to adapt quickly to the situation at hand, look for new opportunities, challenge convention, and be agile, authentic, and bold. An improvisational leader is adept at building a great collaborative ensemble team, is able to both lead and follow, and has a strong interest in creativity and innovation. A great listener too.

Innovation—Innovation is the introduction of something new, such as a bold idea, a new method, or an advancement to an existing product or idea. Improv supports innovation by training the brain to open to new ideas and ways of seeing things.

Judgment—Judgment may be defined as making a considered decision or forming an opinion through evaluation. A challenge with judgment is that we may form judgments based on limited knowledge and biased views. Improv invites us to suspend judgment as we open to new ways of seeing situations and collaborate with other people to explore a multitude of ideas.

Leader—A leader is a person who leads a group, organization, or country. However, simply because a person is called a "leader," that does not mean that person has acquired strong leadership abilities, which must be actively and consistently honed.

Learning & Development—In an organization, learning and development is a function that provides employees with the skills and knowledge they need to grow in their roles, and to help the company grow as well. Applied Improvisation is an important part of any company L&D plan, as improv provides an experiential way for people to adopt a "Yes, and" attitude. Improv is a team skill that can be applied to many workplace training situations, such as overall communication and creativity development.

Learning Objectives—Learning objectives are statements that describe the essential learning that participants of a training have achieved. In Applied Improvisation, the exercises may be customized to match client objectives. During the training or workshop, after each exercise, and as a debrief at the end, learning objectives may be stated to show how the exercises support the intended learning outcomes.

Let's "Yes, And" This (or That)—To me, "Yes, and" is also a verb. An action. An activity. You won't find this phrase in any dictionary (yet!). Think of this phrase as a way to guide your communication with yourself and other people. For example, when you have a different point of view, want to brainstorm, or are embarking on a conversation that requires tact and diplomacy, how about starting with "Let's 'Yes, and' this." Here, you can apply the foundational principle of improv to your interaction. What is the "this" or "that" part? "This" is a more intimate word, closer to the chest. You can feel it when you say it . . . it's close at hand. On the other hand, "that" is a little farther away—you are discussing a topic that's more outside of you. "Let's 'Yes, and' this or that" . . . try it out.

Low-Vibe—Low-vibe communication happens when there is a focus on the problem in every idea, when people are quick to criticize rather than listen, or when people judge other people harshly. Low-vibers tend to think they are always right, and they are discouraging and pessimistic.

Mindfulness—When you are mindful, you are conscious or aware of something. The practice of mindfulness is around letting go, acceptance, trust, patience, nonjudgment. Improv is a great way to engage in mindfulness, as you are encouraged to see situations in a new light, while releasing judgment and embracing acceptance and trust.

Moment-by-Moment Practice—A moment-by-moment practice means you keep returning your attention to the present moment and seek to observe yourself with awareness. This practice is associated with mindfulness, as it involves paying attention to your thoughts and feelings without judgment, and focusing on your surrounding environment with an alert curiosity. Improv supports this approach, as you learn to stay in the moment and practice awareness and observation techniques.

No—The word "No" is an important and valuable word that helps you set boundaries, gives people clarity around what they can expect from you, and lets you stop or shut down situations or events. The word "No" is not as helpful when you want to open to collaboration, brainstorming, or team building. During these times, the word "No" can be negative, and may be an attempt to control the situation.

Nonverbal—Your posture, facial expressions, and eye contact are nonverbal. Nonverbal is communication that is not related to words or speech. Yet, as improv teaches, your nonverbal communication is a powerful way for you to explore the nonverbal cues you are relaying to the world and become aware of how you present yourself.

Observing, or Observation—When observing, you are noticing and perceiving your surroundings. In improv, observing another person's verbal and nonverbal cues, for example, helps you respond with focus, concentration, and attention. You can also observe yourself and how you show up in a particular moment or situation. Getting into the habit of observing contributes to awareness and overall presence.

Paraphrasing—When you paraphrase, you listen to the words of another person and then repeat those words back in slightly different language. Basically, you restate someone else's thoughts or ideas in your own words. Improv practices the art of paraphrasing to encourage you to listen carefully and help show that the other person has been heard. Paraphrasing is an effective communication tool.

Perfectionism—A perfectionist is someone who believes that everything must be flawless and perfect. This person demands an extremely high level of performance that is unachievable. Sometimes, perfectionism can lead both the perfectionist and those around the person to shut down and stop contributing, since they can never get anything right. The practice of improv shows that letting go of perfectionism and embracing failure leads to growth and improvement.

Perspective Taking—Understanding how a situation appears to another person, and holding space for that person's emotional and cognitive reaction is the key here. Perspective taking is different from empathy, since the empathetic person has the ability to share the feelings of another. Both approaches are equally relevant and can be applied to different situations.

Positive Disruptor—A positive disruptor invites courageous conversations that may not be comfortable, in order to challenge the status quo or shift organizational trends that are in need of change.

Play, Playful, or Playfulness—In the context of this book, the focus is on the importance of play for adults. By being playful, you release endorphins, improve brain function, and enhance creativity. Play also helps you manage stress and cope better, and improves mood and overall well-being. Improv and play are closely associated, since improv creates laughter and fun, as you also engage in deep learning.

Practice—When you engage in a practice, you are carrying out or performing an exercise or habit on a regular basis. The goal of maintaining a practice is to improve your knowledge or skill, and as a result, uplevel your life.

Psychological Safety—In the workplace, psychological safety may be defined as an environment that makes individuals feel safe when taking interpersonal risks, and at the same time, supports and recognizes individuals for their contributions and ideas.

Presence—The traditional meaning of presence is simply that you are present, or there. In the context of this book and improv, to be present is to be fully engaged in the moment, to apply active listening and awareness to your situation, and to practice not thinking about other things while you serve the improv experience. Improv creates presence because you must listen, and there isn't any other place you can be when improvising, except present.

Purpose—In the workplace, a sense of purpose is achieved when people get a sense of fulfillment, as they take part in work that is meaningful to them.

Role-Playing—When role-playing, you take on a certain role and enact different scenarios or outcomes, whether with the help of a conversational script or through spontaneous conversation. Role-playing is effective when you want to explore how you communicate with customers, for example. As a team, you can take turns being the team member and the customer to try out different approaches to customer interaction.

Self-Awareness—When you practice self-awareness, you become mindful of your presence and are able to clearly view your strengths and weaknesses, values, desires, and passions. You have a clear understanding of your emotional and mental well-being, including the affect you have on other people. You also gain a view of how people see you, and are able to practice empathy and perspective taking skills. Improv helps people get in touch with self-awareness, since you gain the awareness and observation skills through experiential work, which guides you to greater self-awareness.

Status—In improv, status is about the power difference in the relationship between two or more people. Exercises that invite you to practice status are valuable, as they help you get in touch with how you show up at work and in your life. Status exercises contribute to confidence-building, self-awareness, and an overall improvement in effective communication skills.

Storytelling—The ability to tell stories is a valuable life and work skill. Improv teaches you to tell impromptu stories on the spot and lets you practice getting comfortable quickly accessing stories. This technique supports networking, interviewing, presentation, and sales skills, to give just a few examples.

Team Building—Team building is defined as participating in new activities that teach your team new skills. When you are learning new skills through improv as a team, such as leadership, presentation, and sales development skills, you are a part of a team building experience.

Team Bonding—Team Bonding is all about having fun, collaborating, and strengthening your team's interpersonal relationships. When it comes to the laughter and play of improv, team bonding is a natural outcome.

"Thinking on Your Feet" Skills—Improv is well-known to support "thinking on your feet" skills, which reflect your ability to think and react quickly. You learn to engage audiences, tell stories, gain confidence, and keep calm under pressure.

Toxic Leadership—A toxic leader does not listen to feedback, is arrogant, may discriminate against employees and show a biases or favouritism, likes hierarchy, is often self-interested, or displays an out-of-control ego, as a few examples. A toxic boss has a "my way or the highway" approach, as they like to be right, and are not highly collaborative or effective communicators.

Training the Brain—Studies show that improv techniques activate a flow state by accessing in-the-moment focus which allows you to be "in the zone." For example, a famed 2008 study by neuroscientist Charles Limb shows that when jazz musicians improvise, the part of the brain that is like your inner critic—the dorsolateral prefrontal cortex—decreases in activity, and the part of your brain that accesses creativity—the medial prefrontal cortex—increases. The point: Improv lets you access a part of your brain that focuses your attention, suspends judgment, and expands creativity.

Trust—Trust is often defined as an attitude or feeling that is built, typically over time, through a consistent relationship of honesty and integrity with another person or group. In improv, trust is created as people learn to "have each other's back" through shared experiences. Improv helps build trust through a "give and receive" during exercises, where you are "in it together," being vulnerable and experiencing the risks that come from spontaneous, in-the-moment interactions.

"Yes, And"— "Yes, and" is the foundational principle of improv. When we apply "Yes, and" to our conversations, it means we are applying active listening skills. We are accepting the idea that another person is giving, and building on that offer with our idea. We may agree or we may not agree with what a person is saying, yet we are hearing them. "Yes, and" leads to a greater understanding between people, as you suspend judgment in favor of sharing ideas.

Verbal—Verbal may be defined as spoken communication. In improv, we shine a light on the interactions we have with people every day, and how our verbal skills can lead to more effective communication.

Workplace Culture—Workplace culture may be defined as the shared values, beliefs, and attitudes of people who work together in an organization. Through improv techniques, leaders and teams can establish a set of values or engage in brainstorming sessions to access creative ideas. When you choose to "Yes, and" your company communication, people feel inspired and included in decisions. Improv has the ability to uplevel any workplace culture.

REFERENCES

Aarons-Mele, Morra. "We Need to Talk More About Mental Health at Work." *Harvard Business Review*, November 1, 2018. https:// hbr.org/ 2018/ 11/ we-need-to-talk-more-about-mental-health-at-work.

Cuddy, Amy. "Your Body Language May Shape Who You Are." Filmed June 2012 at TedGlobal 2012, Edinburgh, Scotland. Video, 12:02. __https:// www.youtube.com/ watch?v=Ks-_Mh1QhMc&amp%3Bt=4s.

Brown, Brené. *Dare to Lead: Brave Work. Tough Conversations. Whole Hearts*. New York, NY: Random House, 2018.

Buckingham, Marcus, and Ashley Goodall. "The Power of Hidden Teams." *Harvard Business Review*, May 14, 2019. https://hbr.org/2019/05/the-power-of-hidden-teams.

Cleese, John. *Creativity: A Short and Cheerful Guide*. New York: Crown, 2020.

Clifton, Jon. "The World's Workplace Is Broken—Here's How to Fix It." *Gallup*, June 14, 2022. https:// www.gallup.com/ workplace/393395/world-workplace-broken-fix.aspx.

Dass, Ram. *Be Here Now, Remember*. San Cristobal, NM: Lama Foundation, 1971.

Dickinson, Arlene. *Persuasion: A New Approach to Changing Minds*. Toronto, Ontario, Canada: Collins, 2011.

Felsman, Peter. "Improv Experience Promotes Divergent Thinking, Uncertainty Tolerance, and Affective Well-Being." *Thinking Skills and Creativity* 35 (March 2020). https://doi.org/10.1016/j.tsc.2020.100632.

Gilbert, Elizabeth. *Big Magic: Creative Living Beyond Fear*. New York, Riverhead Books: 2015.

Gino, Francesca. "Using Improv to Unite Your Team." *Harvard Business Review*, May 16, 2019. https://hbr.org/2019/05/using-improv-to-unite-your-team.

Heggie, Betty-Ann. "The Benefits of Laughing in the Office." *Harvard Business Review*, November 16, 2018. https://hbr.org/2018/11/the-benefits-of-laughing-in-the-office.

Ho, Judy. *Stop Self-Sabotage: Six Steps to Unlock Your True Motivation, Harness Your Willpower, and Get Out of Your Own Way*. New York: Harper Wave, 2019.

Joly, Hubert. "How to Lead in the Stakeholder Era." *Harvard Business Review*, May 13, 2021. https://hbr.org/2021/05/how-to-lead-in-the-stakeholder-era.

Jeffers, Susan J. *Feel the Fear and Do It Anyway: Dynamic Techniques for Turning Fear, Indecision, and Anger into Power, Action, and Love*. 20th anniversary edition. New York: Ballantine Books, 2006.

Johnstone, Keith. *Impro: Improvisation and the Theatre*. Abingdon, Oxon, England: Routledge, 2015.

Limb, Charles J., and Allen R. Braun. "Neural Substrates of Spontaneous Musical Performance: An fMRI Study of Jazz

Improvisation." *PLOS ONE* 3, no. 2 (2008). https://journals. plos.org/plosone/article?id=10.1371%2Fjournal.pone.0001679.

LinkedinLearning. *Building the Agile Future: 2023 Workplace Learning Report*. LinkedIn Learning, 2023. https:// learning. linkedin.com/content/dam/me/learning/en-us/pdfs/workplace-learning-report/ LinkedIn-Learning_ Workplace-Learning-Report-2023-EN.pdf.

Lynch, Dudley, and Paul L. Kordis. *Strategy of the Dolphin: Scoring a Win in a Chaotic World*. Fawcett Columbine, 1990.

Nazish, Noma. "How to De-Stress in 5 Minutes or Less, according to a Navy SEAL." *Forbes*, May 30, 2019. https://www. forbes.com/sites/nomanazish/2019/05/30/how-to-de-stress-in-5-minutes-or-less-according-to-a-navy-seal.

Newberg, Andrew, and Mark Waldman. "Why This Word Is So Dangerous to Say or Hear." *Word Can Change Your* Brain (blog). *Psychology Today*, August 1, 2012. https://www.psychologytoday. com/ca/blog/words-can-change-your-brain/201208/why-word-is-so-dangerous-say-or-hear.

Spolin, Viola. *Theater Games for the Classroom: A Teacher's Handbook*, edited by Max Schafer. Northwestern University Press, 2003.

Tolle, Eckhart. *Stillness Speaks*. Vancouver, BC: Namaste Pub; Novato, CA: New World Library, 2003.

Tolle, Eckhart. *The Power of Now: A Guide to Spiritual Enlightenment*. Vancouver, BC, and Novato, CA: Namaste Pub, 1999.

Watts, Alan. *The Book on the Taboo Against Knowing Who You Are*. Vintage Books, New York. 1966.

ACKNOWLEDGMENTS

In 2015, Ralph MacLeod, a friend and colleague of mine in Toronto's improv community since the 1990s, approached me with an intriguing idea: to manage the corporate improv events for his theater. Before long, it became evident that our collaboration was evolving into something more significant— our very own company. Yes Unlimited was born. Ralph, a true wizard in the realms of improv teaching and performance, and I, with my blend of business and improv experience, discovered that we formed a remarkably synergistic partnership. Ralph, I extend my heartfelt thanks to you for not only being an incredible friend and colleague but also for that fateful coffee invitation.

Throughout this Yes Unlimited adventure, many people have facilitated, trained, and collaborated with us and have been an incredible source of support. When I think of our early days, two extraordinary individuals immediately come to mind: the exceptionally talented Jennine Profeta and Dave Pearce, a beloved couple in the improv world. Their contributions were pivotal to our early success. I also want to express my gratitude to Kerry Griffin, a stellar improviser facilitator widely recognized as one of the best in the business. His professionalism consistently enhances every event he participates in. And a special shout-out to Lisa Merchant, one of the most outstanding improvisers anywhere, who famously believes that 'improv can save the world.' Lisa, I wholeheartedly share your belief. We're all in this together.

A special and wholehearted thank you to the eloquent and talented Catherine Gregory, her equally charming partner, Nathan Joblin, and the whole team at Modern Wisdom Press. This book was born through their publishing company, which focuses on publishing books for and by conscious leaders. Your work is a gift to the world. Thanks for the stellar vision, expert guidance, and profound wisdom as we traveled this pathway together. Thank you. Thank you. Thank you.

I want to thank my daughter Allysha Porter (my favorite person in the world), who was this book's first reader and offered her insight and wisdom. She also contributed by helping create the bibliography and charts. I love you. Additional heartfelt thanks go to my first book readers (thank you for all your suggestions, your ideas, and your patience), who all helped shape this book into something better: Catherine Clark, Jude Klassen, Ralph MacLeod, Allysha Porter, and Michele Wright.

Thank you to my friends and family, who are the cornerstone of life. You know who you are. And to my improv collaborators over the years, including my first group in the early 1990s, The Cherry Pop Tarts, and everyone from and associated with The Canadian Space Opera Company, the Toronto-based improv ensemble I was a part of from 2000–2011. The memories of creating two Toronto Fringe shows, *Casa De Los Fantasmas* and *Gravestone Posse*, as well as a six-episode Radio series all at CIUT Radio (University of Toronto), not to mention the live, four-part serial *Peril from Beyond Space* performed at the first Bad Dog Theatre, will stay with me always. And Toronto's improv community, where I have attended countless improv classes, met hundreds of fellow improv enthusiasts, and learned how improv really is a life skill that lets you play while you learn. Thank you to the Speaker Slam family and my friends and collaborators at the Applied Improvisation Network (AIN), a family of Applied Improvisers spreading the message of nonperformance improv techniques around the world. Life is an improv, after all, and if you can laugh while you learn, isn't that a grand way to be?

THANK YOU, DEAR LEADER

Continuing Your "Yes, And" Business Evolution

You've completed the journey of reading this book, and now you're on the path to becoming an improvisational leader. How exciting. You may be wondering where to go next. This adventure is an experiential exploration, after all. You've been invited to commence not only an individual "Yes, and" pilgrimage—which is the "inside job" of what it means to be a "Yes, and" leader—yet also to invite your team and company along on the expedition. As a thank you from me, I invite you to connect with me directly, so I can provide you with some helpful tools.

Scan this link to receive tools to help on your "Yes, And" Individual Quest:

Scan this link to receive tools to help on your "Yes, And" Leadership Quest:

Scan this link to receive tools to help on your "Yes, And" Team Quest:

Scan this link receive tools to help on your "Yes, And" Company Quest:

Made in United States
Troutdale, OR
05/30/2024

20226087R10137